NEW DIRECTIONS FOR ADULT AND CONTINUING EDUCATION

Susan Imel, *Ohio State University*
EDITOR-IN-CHIEF

Collaborative Inquiry as a Strategy for Adult Learning

Lyle Yorks
Columbia University

Elizabeth Kasl
California Institute of Integral Studies

EDITORS

Number 94, Summer 2002

JOSSEY-BASS
San Francisco

COLLABORATIVE INQUIRY AS A STRATEGY FOR ADULT LEARNING
Lyle Yorks, Elizabeth Kasl (eds.)
New Directions for Adult and Continuing Education, no. 94
Susan Imel, Editor-in-Chief

Microfilm copies of issues and articles are available in 16mm and 35mm, as well as microfiche in 105mm, through University Microfilms Inc., 300 North Zeeb Road, Ann Arbor, Michigan 48106-1346.

ISSN 1052-2891   electronic ISSN 1536-0717   ISBN 0-7879-6322-4

NEW DIRECTIONS FOR ADULT AND CONTINUING EDUCATION is part of The Jossey-Bass Higher and Adult Education Series and is published quarterly by Wiley Subscription Services, Inc., a Wiley company, at Jossey-Bass, 989 Market Street, San Francisco, California 94103-1741. Periodicals postage paid at San Francisco, California, and at additional mailing offices. Postmaster: Send address changes to New Directions for Adult and Continuing Education, Jossey-Bass, 989 Market Street, San Francisco, California, 94103-1741.

SUBSCRIPTIONS cost $65.00 for individuals and $135.00 for institutions, agencies, and libraries.

EDITORIAL CORRESPONDENCE should be sent to the Editor-in-Chief, Susan Imel, ERIC/ACVE, 1900 Kenny Road, Columbus, Ohio 43210-1090. e-mail: imel.l@osu.edu.

Cover photograph by Wernher Krutein/PHOTOVAULT © 1990.

www.josseybass.com

Printed in the United States of America on acid-free recycled paper containing at least 20 percent postconsumer waste.

CONTENTS

EDITORS' NOTES

Our experience with collaborative inquiry (CI) is more than a decade old and is a journey that continues to unfold. As a form of human science research CI embodies epistemological and political values that, though challenging much that goes on in the academy, are highly consistent with principles of adult education, learning, and development. We have come to recognize the power of CI not only as a form of research but also as an approach for facilitating adult learning that creates the necessary conditions for effective discourse and honors multiple ways of knowing.

The CI process involves cycles of action and reflection characterized by open conversation in which experience is shared through whole-person processes, subjected to validity criteria, and disclosed for the public arena. This same process describes how the editors and authors constructed this issue of *New Directions*. For the authors, writing was itself an action, involving reflection on their prior experience with CI. Developing each chapter involved three or four cycles between ourselves and the authors, with each cycle revealing additional meaning from their experience. Because at least one of us was aware of each author's experience, we were able to query and share in the emerging insights. In our own chapters we share what we have learned as beneficiaries of these iterative cycles of mutual reflections.

The cases described in this volume were selected because each involves an innovative use of the CI process. Because of space considerations we have asked the authors to highlight particular aspects of their inquiries. We greatly appreciate their willingness to do so. Hoping to stimulate additional inquiries, we invite readers to consider this volume an invitation to join us in exploring the adult education applications of CI.

Lyle Yorks
Elizabeth Kasl
Editors

1

*Through its structure for peer participation, multiple
ways of knowing, and systematic validity procedures,
collaborative inquiry provides a highly effective strategy
for facilitating learning from experience.*

Collaborative Inquiry for Adult Learning

Elizabeth Kasl, Lyle Yorks

Collaborative inquiry (CI) provides a systematic structure for learning from
experience. Participants organize themselves in small groups to address a
compelling question that brings the group together. In order to construct
new meaning related to their question, collaborative inquirers engage in
cycles of reflection and action, evoke multiple ways of knowing, and practice validity procedures. Typically, they balance exploration of inner experience with action in the world. CI is especially appropriate for pursuing
topics that are professionally developmental or socially controversial or that
require personal or social healing. These categories are of course not mutu-
ally exclusive and are representative of the kinds of learning challenges that
confront adults in the complex, highly turbulent and diverse world of the
twenty-first century.

The purpose of this volume is to demonstrate through case example the
power of collaborative inquiry as a facilitative structure for adult learning.
Eight profiles of collaborative inquiry learning projects demonstrate a broad
range of inquiry objectives and outcomes. Before saying more about the
projects themselves, we describe collaborative inquiry processes and origins.

Collaborative Inquiry Is Part of a Larger Family

Collaborative inquiry is one among many inquiry methodologies that are
experience-based and action-oriented. Other strategies commonly included
in this group are action research, action inquiry, action learning, action science, and participatory action research. Ann Brooks and Karen Watkins

NEW DIRECTIONS FOR ADULT AND CONTINUING EDUCATION, no. 94, Summer 2002 © Wiley Periodicals, Inc.

(1994) point out that these various strategies have several characteristics in common. Each is intended to create new knowledge drawn systematically from the life experience of persons most centrally involved in the context of the inquiry. Newly created knowledge becomes the basis of new action that is intended to create change in professional practice, organizational outcomes, or social democracies (pp. 11–12). Although this family of inquiry methodologies has for decades been part of the discourse about qualitative research methods, only recently have adult educators begun to recognize that these research methods are excellent organizing structures for adult learning (Quigley and Kuhne, 1997; Bray, Lee, Smith, and Yorks, 2000).

As with many newly emerging concepts, the idea of a family of experience-based, action-oriented inquiry strategies has manifested with different names and slightly varying profiles. Brooks and Watkins (1994) name this family "action inquiry technologies." Writing for a management audience, Joe Raelin (1999) extends Brooks and Watkins' work but chooses the umbrella designation "action strategies." Over the course of two decades, Peter Reason has chosen several labels to designate this group of research approaches—"human inquiry" and "new paradigm research" (Reason and Rowan, 1981; Reason, 1988, 1994a), "collaborative inquiry" (Reason, 1990), "participative inquiry" (Reason, 1994b), and most recently "action research" (Reason and Bradbury, 2001).

In this volume we use the term *collaborative inquiry* to refer to one specific strategy among the many that belong to this family of strategies. We ascribe to the term a context of adult learning and borrow a definition from adult educators, "Collaborative inquiry is a systematic process [for learning from personal experience] consisting of repeated episodes of reflection and action through which a group of peers strives to answer a question of importance to them" (Bray, Lee, Smith, and Yorks, 2000, p. 6).

Collaborative inquiry rests on principles articulated by Reason (1988) and John Heron (1996) when they write about a process that they now call "co-operative inquiry." Our use of the term *collaborative,* in contrast to *co-operative,* has a historical explanation. We chose that term in 1991, when a plethora of labels for experience-based, action-oriented methods was in play. At the time, Reason was using the term "collaborative inquiry" as a more general and inclusive designation than the specific set of procedures that he called "co-operative inquiry"; it made sense to us to embrace the more general definition, in part because information about co-operative inquiry was relatively sparse. As we developed our inquiry projects, more information about co-operative inquiry emerged (Reason, 1994a; Heron, 1996; Heron and Reason 1997, 2001). We saw that our practice of collaborative inquiry was similar to co-operative inquiry. Although we currently make some distinctions, they are beyond the scope of this volume. We continue to use our label *collaborative inquiry,* while adopting the term *CI* as a convention in the book, by which we intentionally connote collaborative or co-operative inquiry.

Heron and Reason (2001) stress that co-operative inquiry involves researching *with* people, rather than conducting research *on* them or *about* them. Intrinsic to co-operative inquiry are two fundamental participatory principles. First, each inquirer participates actively in his or her own meaning-making by using processes that ground new knowledge in personal experience. Second, each inquirer participates fully in all decisions that affect the inquiry. These two participatory principles in combination make co-operative inquiry unique among the family of experience-based, action-oriented approaches to research.

To clarify the unique quality of co-operative or collaborative inquiry (CI), we compare it to the strategy typically called "action research." Action research has long been familiar to organizational change agents (Elden and Levin, 1991; Elden and Chisholm, 1993) and represents a rapidly growing interest among educational researchers (Quigley and Kuhne, 1997; Zeichner, 2001).

The purpose of action research is to change the system; the process is driven by a problem in the system. Action researchers gather information from many different sources within their environment for purposes of analysis and intervention. The action research team focuses its learning goals on the system. In contrast, the purpose of CI is for members of the inquiry group to change themselves. In response to a sense of personal disquiet or disorienting dilemma, an individual invites others with similar interests to join an inquiry. Together, inquirers formulate a compelling question that they can answer by examining "data" from their personal experience. Their goal is to develop their own capacities, either personal or professional.

For example, a typical action research question might be posed by a group of educational administrators as, How can we improve the way that teachers use technology in the classroom? A CI question posed by this same group of administrators might be, How can we improve our ability as administrators to influence the way teachers use technology in the classroom? The focus of the action research question is on changing the system directly, whereas the CI question focuses on the inquirers themselves as the primary target for learning and change. Of course, changes in the inquirers may lead to changes in the system. The difference, although it may seem minor, is radically significant. CI shifts the learners' focus away from others and to themselves.

How Learning Happens in Collaborative Inquiry

By sharing power and responsibility equally and following explicit validity practices in mutual pursuit of new meaning, participants create a learning structure that mirrors the conditions long held by adult educators as fundamental to communicative learning—freedom from coercion, equality of access to information, and norms of inquiry that reinforce commitment to building shared meaning through consensual validity testing (Mezirow, 1991, 2000). Indeed, a major contribution that CI makes to adult education theory and practice is its systematic structure for processes through which these idealized conditions are realized.

Two processes warrant explanation—implementing a wholistic epistemology and attending to validity.

Multiple Ways of Knowing for Whole-Person Learning. One of the participatory research principles advocated by Heron and Reason (1997, 2001) requires that knowledge construction be grounded solidly in personal experience. They describe an extended epistemology consisting of four ways of knowing—experiential, presentational, propositional, and practical. Experiential knowing is evident when we meet and feel the presence of some energy, entity, person, place, process, or thing. Presentational knowing is expressed in graphic, plastic, moving, musical, and verbal art forms. Propositional knowing is formulated by intellectual statements, both verbal and numeric, organized with logic and evidence. Practical knowing is evident in knowing how to exercise a skill (Heron, 1996, p. 33). Heron configures the relationship among the four ways of knowing as a pyramid and uses the term "up-hierarchy" (1992, pp. 20–21) to describe how what is above is grounded in what is below. Thus, experiential knowing is the base of all learning and grounds all other forms of knowing. Practical knowing is at the pinnacle.

Given the premise that new knowledge must be grounded in experiential knowing, the challenge that confronts a group of would-be knowledge makers is, How can we share our individual experiential knowing in ways that make it accessible to group members, so that we can construct new knowledge as a group?

Responding to the challenge, Heron (1992, 1996) has developed a full-bodied theory describing how people connect their multiple ways of knowing. Presentational knowing, which is rooted in the imaginal and expressed through intuition and imagery, provides a pathway that connects experiential knowing (which is nonlinguistic) with propositional knowing (which is linguistic). Similarly, Peter Reason and Peter Hawkins (1988) have examined the dialectic relationship between paths of expression and paths of explanation. Co-operative inquiry groups spend considerable time in coming to know their data set (which is the lived experience of each group member) through presentational or expressive modes of knowing before moving to reflection, analysis, and meaning-making.

To illustrate the process, we return to the case of our hypothetical educational administrators who ask, How can we improve our ability as administrators to influence the way teachers use technology in the classroom? Stepping inside the research frame explicated by Heron and Reason, we imagine how the administrator-researchers might follow the two participatory principles: grounding research findings in their own experience rather than the experience of others, and sharing equally all decisions related to their research.

The template for their research procedure is thus. As co-researchers, after identifying mutual interest and formulating a research question, the group designs a research plan, asking, What data shall we collect? Because they are required to collect the "data of their own experience," they agree on actions that each member can take in order to create personal experience that relates to the group's inquiry question. When the group adjourns, the inquirers shift their role from being co-researchers to being co-subjects. By carrying out the actions to which all have agreed, members generate personal experiences that will become the research group's "data." When the group convenes to make meaning of members' collective experiences, it must first learn what the experiences are. However, the quality of one person's lived experience is not easily communicated to another. Thus, the challenge before the group is, How do we communicate to each other our experience as co-subjects so that we can make sense of it as co-researchers?

In the case of the educational administrators, they spent their first meeting sharing personal perspectives on why each person is drawn to the inquiry. They notice from their stories that each administrator feels underskilled with technology. Further, each at times feels uncomfortable when communicating with teachers and state-level bureaucrats. Curious about possible patterns in their discomfort, they decide that for the group's first action, each administrator will watch for personal signs of discomfort and record them in a journal.

When the group reconvenes, its task is to share members' experience with discomfort so that the group can construct meaning from members' collective experience. Recognizing the challenge of relating personal experience in ways that make it accessible to others, the group turns to a presentational mode of knowing. After reviewing their journal notes, administrators spend time quietly creating watercolor sketches that express their personal moments of discomfort. When the group moves to "examining its data," each administrator describes his or her experience of discomfort, using the visual art as a supporting prop. After the full "data set" is before the group, that is, after each person has described his or her experience, the group then reflects on patterns of meaning in the collective stories. The inquirers discern a possible pattern: members' discomfort seems most acute when they are talking with a teacher they perceive as relatively competent with technology. The group decides that for its next action, each member will seek out a technologically competent teacher and ask that teacher to convene a lunchtime technology discussion with other teachers. The administrator's primary participation during the discussion will be to ask clarifying questions. Journal observations will continue; the next action-reflection cycle is set in motion.

Validity Processes for Making Meaning. When learners make meaning from their own experience, the question arises, How can the validity of this knowledge be judged? According to Heron and Reason (Heron, 1988; Heron and Reason, 1997, 2001), the primary criterion is coherence. Each participant should experience intrapersonal coherence among the four ways of knowing; that is, propositional knowing and practical actions should cohere and should not contradict the learner's own sense of felt experience or presentational construal. Further, co-inquirers should experience coherence among themselves in relation to their mutual findings. This interinquirer agreement is consensual validation, described by Mezirow (1991) as the essential element in communicative learning.

Heron and Reason, throughout the years, have described a number of validity procedures that can assist inquirers with practicing "critical subjectivity" (Heron, 1996; Heron and Reason, 1997, 2001), a term they use to refer to rigorous practice for examining how one's own subjective experience can be the basis for "high-quality" (2001, p. 184) knowing. Chief among the validity procedures are using multiple research cycles, sustaining authentic collaboration, challenging consensus collusion, managing distress, and creating balance between divergence and convergence, chaos and order, and reflection and action. Other practices include use of action science methods for avoiding defensive routines and group think (Bray and others, 2000).

Careful attentiveness to validity procedures provides rigor to the process and builds trust in the meaning that is constructed. Engaging in these procedures can be both energizing and painful. The commitment of group members to inquiry that is authentic, open to multiple ways of knowing, and marked by a desire for avoiding self-deception is essential to the CI process. These qualities are evident in the inquiries reported in this book.

Inquiries That Follow

The chapters that follow provide insight into how collaborative inquiry provides structure for learning. Taken as a group they demonstrate diversity of purpose, context, organization, and roles played by the adult educator. They also illustrate how to use multiple ways of knowing and validity procedures. Our objective is to provide guidance to adult educators while also adding to the emerging discourse about collaborative and co-operative inquiry.

Each project created a complex learning experience for its participants, the fullness of which cannot be captured within the space limits of this volume. As editors familiar with each project, we asked authors to highlight particular characteristics of their projects so that this volume, taken as a whole, would represent the diversity of issues that we believe are important to adult educators. We also asked each author to tell an engaging story, hoping that each chapter might evoke in the reader a felt sense of the CI experience.

For easy reference, we provide a brief profile at the beginning of each chapter that gives an overview of the project's participants, purpose, and outcomes. Most chapters use direct quotations from the learners themselves. Chapter authors have audio recordings of the inquiry meetings from which these quotations are drawn. Chapters Five and Seven use participants' real names; all other chapters use pseudonyms.

In Chapter Two, "Making Sense of One's Experience in the Workplace," Suzanne Van Stralen writes about an inquiry involving nursing managers who are an intact workgroup. Suzanne is an adult educator who assists organizations with staff development; she met with the nurses at the hospital during their shift, helping them with their inquiry about wholistic ways of being in the workplace. Her account provides an example of CI in which the educator is not a primary participant.

Chapter Three, "Using the Power of Collaborative Inquiry: Community Women Learn and Lead Themselves," describes an inquiry by community women who work together as peer counselors for breastfeeding. Diverse ethnically and racially, the peer counselors discover that their growing capacity to communicate across cultural difference is a valuable skill that they can use as consultants to community organizations. As a group, these inquirers have less education than participants in the other projects described in this volume. Linda Smith, a community and organizational development consultant, initiated this project. Like Suzanne, Linda approached an intact group of which she was not a member.

Chapters Four and Five report projects in which the initiating educator is a fully participating member. Both chapters describe inquiries that pursue elusive yet powerful phenomena of inner experience for purposes of ultimately enhancing the inquirers' practice and presence in the world. In Chapter Four, "Nurturing Intuition Through Group Learning," Annette Weinberg Zelman relates the experience of community college faculty and administrators whose inquiry purpose was to claim and nurture their own intuitive capacities. In Chapter Five, "Midwife to a Learning Community: Spirit as Co-inquirer," Whitney Wherrett Roberson and her colleagues report their experience as professional religious leaders who developed their capacities to support learning community and transformation in others.

The next two chapters continue with CI groups in which the initiators are full participants. Both describe the experience of women who use CI to confront marginalization, oppression, and internalized oppression. In Chapter Six, "Exploring Internalized Oppression and Healing Strategies," Penny Rosenwasser draws generously from her audiotapes to bring readers inside the conversation of Jewish women learning to recognize and heal from their own internalized anti-Semitism. In Chapter Seven, "Weaving Our Stories as They Weave Us," Cecilia Pritchard and Pamelaia Sanders describe how women scholars of color experience CI as cultural praxis. Confronting the challenges of being graduate students in an institution that is overwhelmingly dominated by white Western hegemony, these women affirm that education for them is a form of social activism and their capacity to sustain their studies requires them to infuse their experience with spirituality.

The last two chapters profile projects in which several CI groups are created within a single organization. In Chapter Eight, "A Multiple-Group Inquiry into Whiteness," the authors describe an ongoing cultural consciousness project sponsored within a small university. With the intention of translating new awareness into personal behavior change and social action, participants of white European descent learn how their dominant position in society limits their thinking and behavior. Beyond its valuable contribution to an area of adult learning that is increasingly recognized for its social importance, this chapter also merits attention because it provides a model for creating architecture that supports multiple groups with a single inquiry purpose. In Chapter Nine, "Uniting Teacher Learning: Collaborative Inquiry for Professional Development," John N. Bray describes another multiple-group CI initiative, this one involving teachers within a rural school district. John is an adult educator with staff development responsibilities in the school, where he is also a science teacher. John negotiated with the administration to use CI as an alternative to traditional methods of in-service teacher training and development.

Working with the authors of these various cases has proven to be a valuable experience for us, revealing new insights into the nuances of initiating and facilitating CI. In Chapter Ten we highlight the lessons we have drawn from these cases.

References

Bray, J., Lee, J., Smith, L. L., and Yorks, L. *Collaborative Inquiry in Practice: Action, Reflection, and Making Meaning.* Thousand Oaks, Calif.: Sage, 2000.

Brooks, A., and Watkins, K. "A New Era for Action Technologies: A Look at the Issues." In A. Brooks and K. Watkins (eds.), *The Emerging Power of Action Inquiry Technologies.* New Directions for Adult Education and Continuing Education, no. 63. San Francisco: Jossey-Bass, 1994.

Elden, M., and Chisholm, R. F. "Emerging Varieties of Action Research: Introduction to the Special Issue." *Human Relations,* 1993, *46* (2), 121–141.

Elden, M., and Levin, M. "Co-generative Learning: Bringing Participation into Action Research." In W. F. Whyte (ed.), *Participatory Action Research.* Newbury Park, Calif.: Sage, 1991.

Heron, J. "Validity in Co-operative Inquiry." In P. Reason (ed.), *Human Inquiry in Action: Developments in New Paradigm Research.* Newbury Park, Calif.: Sage, 1988.

Heron, J. *Feeling and Personhood: Psychology in Another Key.* Newbury Park, Calif.: Sage, 1992.

Heron, J. *Co-operative Inquiry: Research into the Human Condition.* Thousand Oaks, Calif.: Sage, 1996.

Heron, J., and Reason, P. "A Participatory Inquiry Paradigm." *Qualitative Inquiry,* 1997, *3* (3), 274–294.

Heron, J., and Reason, P. "The Practice of Co-operative Inquiry: Research 'With' Rather than 'On' People." In P. Reason and H. Bradbury, (eds.), *Handbook of Action Research.* Thousand Oaks, Calif.: Sage, 2001.

Mezirow, J. *Transformative Dimensions of Adult Learning.* San Francisco: Jossey-Bass, 1991.

Mezirow, J. "Thinking Like an Adult." In J. Mezirow and Associates, *Learning as Transformation.* San Francisco: Jossey-Bass, 2000.

Quigley, B. A., and Kuhne, G. W. (eds.). *Creating Practical Knowledge Through Action Research: Posing Problems, Solving Problems, and Improving Daily Practice.* New Directions for Adult Education and Continuing Education, no. 73. San Francisco: Jossey-Bass, 1997.

Raelin, J. "Preface." In Raelin, J. (ed.), Special Issue: *The Action Dimension in Management: Diverse Approaches to Research, Teaching, and Development. Management Learning,* 1999, *30* (2), 115–125.

Reason, P. (ed.). *Human Inquiry in Action: Developments in New Paradigm Research.* Newbury Park, Calif.: Sage, 1988.

Reason, P. "Editorial." *Collaborative Inquiry,* 1990, *1* (1), 1.

Reason, P. (ed.). *Participation in Human Inquiry.* Thousand Oaks, Calif.: Sage, 1994a.

Reason, P. "Three Approaches to Participative Inquiry." In N. Denzin and Y. Lincoln (eds.), *Handbook of Qualitative Research.* Thousand Oaks, Calif.: Sage, 1994b.

Reason, P., and Bradbury, H. "Introduction: Inquiry and Participation in Search of a World Worthy of Human Aspiration." In P. Reason and H. Bradbury (eds.), *Handbook of Action Research.* Thousand Oaks, Calif.: Sage, 2001.

Reason, P., and Hawkins, P. "Storytelling as Inquiry." In P. Reason (ed.), *Human Inquiry in Action: Developments in New Paradigm Research.* Newbury Park, Calif.: Sage, 1988.

Reason, P., and Rowan, J. (eds.). *Human Inquiry: A Sourcebook of New Paradigm Research.* New York: Wiley, 1981.

Zeichner, K. "Educational Action Research." In P. Reason and H. Bradbury, (eds.), *Handbook of Action Research.* Thousand Oaks, Calif.: Sage, 2001.

ELIZABETH KASL *is professor of transformative learning at the California Institute of Integral Studies in San Francisco and a founding member of three learning collaboratives.*

LYLE YORKS *is associate professor of adult education at Teachers College, Columbia University, where he is director of the Adult Education Guided Intensive Study (AEGIS) doctoral program.*

2

Six nursing managers learn to be more wholistic in how they manage responsibilities in a fast-paced work environment oriented toward cost efficiency.

Making Sense of One's Experience in the Workplace

Suzanne Van Stralen

Participants: Six nursing managers and one independent organizational consultant. The nurses, five women and one man, are responsible for patient care services in an acute care hospital. The consultant convened the group, designed the learning program, and is the author of this chapter.

Inquiry purpose: To heal fragmentation and separation.

Inquiry question: How do we communicate in order to promote a culture of mutual respect and cohesiveness among management and staff from all departments, shifts, and facilities?

Process: Eight cycles of reflection and action in five months. Reflection sessions were four hours, scheduled at two-week intervals.

Outcomes: Participants expanded their thinking and action to include valuing personal relationships, authenticity in communication, and work practices that promote community among themselves and with their staff. Participants demonstrated empowered leadership by taking action that resulted in a hospitalwide employee recognition celebration.

I have worked for fifteen years as an organizational consultant with major national and international corporations and have repeatedly experienced the consequences of clients relying solely on analysis and logic as a way of functioning. From my perspective, these clients have lost their capacity for full knowing and learning. By suppressing other ways of knowing and relying only on the fragment of their intellect, they limit their capacity to learn from personal experience. Unable to relate in a connected way to their work world, each other, or the world of nature and humanity, they also are separated from their own sense of being. In a work world permeated by a growing sense of isolation, both personal well-being and work performance suffer.

Negotiating Project Arrangements

Based on my experience I wanted to experiment with a learning strategy that would help learners in the workplace change how they are affected by fragmentation and separation. Hoping to convene a CI, I initiated conversations with hospital administrators and the director of patient services in a health care organization in Northern California where I had worked successfully as an organizational development specialist.

After receiving permission to present the proposed activity to approximately thirty nursing managers, I succeeded in recruiting six volunteers who made a commitment to engage in eight reflection-action cycles. From June through October, the six managers and I met in comfortable conference rooms located on the hospital campus. Each reflection session was scheduled for four hours during paid work time.

Although my introduction to the nursing managers was facilitated through hospital administration, the learning program I designed was not presented as an organization development intervention with outcome accountability to administration. After providing an introduction to nursing managers, administration stepped back from further involvement. The managers contracted directly with me for the learning program and negotiated their release time with the head of their department. They had complete freedom to decide what, if anything, they would share with others about their learning. Although this arrangement may sound unusual to some administrators, because the hospital had been cutting back on training for cost containment reasons, the administration was perhaps particularly open to providing the nursing managers with access to this opportunity. Further, my previous work as a consultant within this system afforded me credibility, and I offered my services without compensation.

Forming the Group

The nursing managers were responsible for the intensive care unit and medical-surgical services. Each was a highly experienced registered nurse (RN) accountable for large budgets and staff. The six had worked as a team for over a year; a seventh team member was unable to participate. Four of the participants were Caucasian; two described themselves as Caucasian-Hispanic and Hispanic-German-English.

Many nurses enter the profession with ideals about providing care in a context of intimate relationships with patients and their families. Today, however, nurses face immense paperwork and financial restraints. At the time of the intervention, these six nurse-managers worked in the midst of a financial turnaround effort. Resources were slim; they confronted cutbacks in personnel and spending. The competitive and financially driven health care environment created tension for the managers, forcing them to balance humanistic values with bottom line decisions. Deb describes the nurses' need for rapid action and high accuracy. "We don't sell or repair machines. We work with human beings who are sick, and errors on our part can be fatal."

Escaping the Hectic Work Environment

I understood that the life-and-death challenges of the work environment would make it difficult for participants to be fully present for the learning program. At the same time, I believed our learning endeavor required that we somehow find a way to interrupt the nurse-managers' habituated modes of rapid problem analysis and fast action. Searching for a strategy that could facilitate transition from the hectic work environment into a peaceful refuge for wholistic learning, I decided on guided visualization.

In the first session I used the symbol of a wooden bridge. Speaking softly, I invited participants to leave the busy hospital behind and to walk over this bridge into the pastoral peace of an apple orchard. As I guided their attention to the sounds of water flowing under the bridge, the smells of the orchard, the feel of warm sun on their faces, I could see participants visibly relax their bodies. Several of them sighed as their breathing became slower and deeper. I used the same visualization at the beginning of each of the first four sessions.

As the inquiry moved forward, all group members expressed a deepening appreciation for our ritual of walking away from the hectic workplace into a soothing environment. By the fifth session they were enthusiastically writing and facilitating their own visualizations with themes of redwood forests, beaches, and desert. Hank talked about how he could not have been open to the learning program without this transition. "I think the guided visualization at the beginning of the sessions was very important. It was a critical element at the beginning of the group to transition because everybody is coming in with all these thoughts racing through their minds. How are you going to be effective with this if you can't help them step away for awhile? I think the guided visualization was very important and is needed to do this work in the corporate setting."

Stimulating the Imaginal and Disrupting Habitual Responses

I used other strategies to help participants break out of habitual ways of thinking and acting. Taking my guidance from John Heron (1996a, 1999) on how to stimulate imagination, I placed a number of objects in the learning environment that would remind people of their connection with nature and beauty. On the heavy oak boardroom table I scattered a silk scarf, a stuffed frog, a Tibetan bell, and a piece of driftwood complete with a bird's nest and air plants.

I invited participants to ring the bells when they experienced insights or fresh thinking. After a few sessions they began to ring the bells on their own initiative. During the seventh session, they enthusiastically rang the bells three times and with laughter and cheers declared that they had experienced a "three-bell meeting."

Participants valued the whimsical, free-flowing thinking that these objects stimulated. Counter to the cultural norms of their work world, these elements of playfulness and beauty released group members from habituated patterns of thinking and acting.

Moving Through Cycles of Reflection and Action

All CI groups move through cycles of reflection and action. At the initial reflection meeting, members explore what the topic means to each participant, and if time allows, they develop an initial question that will guide their inquiry about the topic. They also make logistical decisions, create group guidelines, and develop a confidentiality agreement.

Establishing a culture of equality and safety provided a special challenge for this group because one of its six participants was the supervisor to whom the other five reported. Important first steps toward meeting the challenge included acknowledging and talking openly about this power difference, as well as agreeing to group norms and confidentiality. Thinking later about those first steps, Hank noted, "It was important to the group because when you have a hierarchy, you have a problem."

During the group's first meeting participants set a norm for authentic conversation and discovered the liberatory impact of self-disclosure. The more authentic they became in expressing thoughts and feelings, the more able they became in being personally vulnerable. New voices of honesty came forward and these authentic communications engendered mutual trust.

Everyone talked about how listening to each other's stories helped break their sense of isolation. Kay put it this way: "One of the things for me was around the discussion in the first session when we were talking about what fragmentation and separation meant to us, and how everybody was feeling in regard to that. I think I was feeling I was the one who was totally lost here at work. Or I was feeling like the staff communicate in a way that isn't pleasant, [but just] with me." Kay recalls that for the first time she realized that the other managers shared her feelings. "During that discussion I felt like I was not alone in how I felt."

Telling stories and talking about the topic of fragmentation and separation helped the group develop its initial CI question, "How do we communicate in order to promote a climate of mutual respect and cohesiveness among management and staff?" They then identified their first action, which included developing five questions for a staff survey regarding mutual respect. Group members agreed to record their actions and observations in journals and bring them to the next meeting.

To help the group understand that reflection did not have to rely solely on written or spoken words, I introduced expressive arts. At the second reflection session, I gave each participant a ball of clay and invited them to create sculptures that expressed their experience when they carried out the action. When the sculptures were finished, participants used them as visual props while they described their experiences. This nonverbal reflection with expressive arts and the ensuing dialogue prompted the managers to change their initial orientation toward their topic. From "fixing" their staff through a survey, they moved to exploring themselves and their own work practices. As they developed insight about refocusing the inquiry on themselves, their voices grew more animated and the pace of conversation quickened.

Thinking later about the importance of this day, Ann explained, "This was a perspective shift for everyone. We had started with looking at the staff, looking at other peoples' problems and not our own. It was good when we turned around and started talking about how it wasn't 'them.' It became 'us' and we did some of our better work. Before, we were going out to ask the rest of the staff how we were going to fix them. And finally, we shifted over to making our question more introspective. Then we became more in control of our own actions."

After a period of focusing on their personal capacities for communication and mutual respect, the group began to develop a desire to move their new understanding into the larger system. By the fourth session members began to ask how they could foster community throughout the hospital. They took their idea for hospitalwide employee recognition to hospital administration and persuaded the administrative team to sponsor and fund a recognition day.

Using the Extended Epistemology

Collaborative inquiry invites an extended epistemology in its use of four forms of knowing—beginning with experiential knowing and moving to presentational, propositional, and practical knowing. These forms of knowing precisely mirror the four forms of learning described by Heron (1996b, 1999).

Working with the four ways of knowing helped these nurse-participants create a successful inquiry. The group's growing awareness about the interplay of experiential, presentational, and propositional knowing promoted members' capacity for reflection, thus leading eventually to changes in their thinking and their capacity for practical actions in the work environment.

Participants found it difficult to put into words the experiential knowing they acquired in face-to-face encounters with other people, places, or things in the workplace. I helped them express their experiential knowing from workplace encounters by introducing various presentational forms, such as story, drawing, movement, and clay sculpture. In introducing expressive processes I reassured group members that no judgment would be made about their artwork because it is the process, not the product, that facilitates learning. Participants worked on their presentational pieces individually without talking. Once the participants completed their art work, they described it to the group, linking it with their felt experience during the action phases of the inquiry.

Jan describes her surprise with presentational construal. "It opens up that part of the brain that you don't usually tap into. You usually use your cognition and word processing and not your pictorial processing. So I think it is learning. It is about opening up areas. I was surprised with what other people's pictures came up with. So in this opening up a different area, a light bulb may have come on."

Participants valued presentational activities because those activities deepened members' experience of listening to each other. Hank called this process "relational listening." Kay talked about how sharing through presentational modes promotes an enhanced quality of understanding. "These processes open a door to humanize us. . . . Multiple ways of knowing are a bridge. . . . because they are away from the usual 'talking now and thinking later.' You have to listen to the other side. And they are an offering from the participants. They are really an offering of themselves. They are not the normal. They are a way of offering another piece of themselves and that's a bridge."

Presentational knowing also helps reestablish the connection between members' humanity and emotion. Hank describes the growth of his understanding about the value of bringing emotions into his work practice. "I remember the day that Kay got tearful. I didn't realize. I thought she had on a more sturdy suit of armor. Her being vulnerable like that kind of opened my eyes. I have begun to bring emotions into my work practice. Not as much as I would have liked to this point, but I have started doing this. . . . I have become more comfortable with it, so I am growing there."

Propositional knowing occurs when a CI group makes meaning from members' collective experiences. It was during this meaning-making phase of the reflection sessions that changes in the nurse-managers' conversations became most noticeable. Conversations that were most engaging and productive had a spirit of their own and resulted in fresh ideas and concepts. These powerful group conversations were synergistic as the group's thinking evolved into new collective actions. Group members called these conversations "popping conversations" and talked about their heightened level of energy and enthusiasm. Kay explains, "I think the word to describe them is alive. You are throwing out ideas. The 'popping' is the creativity. I mean it's like popping out ideas. You don't necessarily take every idea. You build. It was like building upon building blocks. Maybe it was more energized. I think it was different from brainstorming. It was a more excited kind of conversation."

It is unclear what caused these generative conversations to develop so fully; however, they were part of something very fresh, creative, and special that opened up changes in thinking and action. Popping conversation began to occur in the fourth reflection session and continued through the eighth.

Although most group time focused on experiential, presentational, and propositional knowing, participants also valued practical knowing and application of their new capacities in the work environment. Marie describes her impression of the value of new work practices. "We started focusing on what we could do, and I guess I was really impressed that the employee recognition celebration came out of this action. . . . I don't think this hospital would ever have done the celebration if it weren't for us."

Developing Self-Directed Learning

In a traditional collaborative inquiry, participants assume primary responsibility for making decisions together about the design and implementation of all of their learning throughout the inquiry. The initiator of the inquiry moves quickly to a peer relationship with group members.

As an organizational development specialist experienced in health care environments, I assessed that this approach would not prove effective as an initial strategy within this organization. Members of this culture are accustomed to expert models in which facilitators or trainers take charge. Participants expect formal direction and logical organization of learning activities. Recognizing these expectations, I knew I should begin the learning program as a traditional facilitator, but I also actively intended to transfer responsibility to the learners.

I planned a number of steps that gradually transferred responsibility and helped participants grow confident in their ability to assume leadership for the process. For example, in the first meeting I took notes about the emerging themes of reflection. In the second meeting I asked for a volunteer to record emerging themes and distribute these notes to all members of the group within five days. At the third meeting I asked for two volunteers who would help plan and facilitate the next meeting. These volunteers met with me by phone. We repeated this pattern for the next two meetings.

Jan explains her perspective on the value of sharing responsibility. "I think facilitating the sessions helped us to validate what we were learning. It also helped me kind of see and have a better understanding by doing. When you are responsible you realize how much understanding you do or don't have. You have to look a little closer. When I was responsible as a facilitator I would think and reflect more about what I was learning. Maybe that was it—more reflection—that I validated what I was learning."

Participants assumed total responsibility for planning and facilitating session seven. In advance of this session I had used the metaphor of soul to talk about the deepening of learning from experience. In planning for the seventh session, the group decided to bring clay flower pots. Modeling what

I had taught them, they played music but did not speak to each other as they decorated the flower pots in a search for expression about the group's soul. After half an hour each person was ready to explain the meaning of what he or she had created. The ensuing discussion uncovered a theme of growth. Members brought the day to a close by observing that although the inquiry had helped them grow significantly they were not yet close to understanding the soul of their team.

Facilitating CI in the Workplace

As I think about my personal experience of bringing CI into the workplace, I discern several factors that I think are important. Because participants must be able to justify investment of time and energy, successful CI in the workplace requires clarity and agreement about the intention of the inquiry, as well as full engagement and commitment by all involved. Inquiry processes may seem unusual to participants as the CI initiator supports activities and processes that encourage participants to move beyond habituated modes of learning and thinking. Although CI rests on a systematic framework, it is not a linear process. Participants must be open to exploring learning processes that use an extended epistemology with expressive arts activities that encourage the imaginal and affective dimensions of learning, critical reflection, and synergistic group conversation. They must be willing to learn gradually how to assume responsibility for planning and facilitating their own learning. Participants should be helped to accept that this learning process will include times of chaos and feelings of confusion. Ambiguity will require flexibility and fluidity with new roles and responsibilities. During a CI, the facilitator and participants move back and forth in these respective roles. Even though the facilitator is not a member of the workplace, she is part of the inquiry group. The blurring of boundaries offers an opportunity for everyone to participate in learning through experience. Engagement depends on development of an egalitarian and trusting relationship among participants as well as with the facilitator.

In describing the nursing managers' inquiry, I have tried to illustrate several dimensions of facilitation that I believe are important when implementing CI in the workplace. I summarize them here:

- Having experience with CI and group dynamics
- Understanding the organizational context
- Supporting a learning culture that values mutual respect, authenticity, trust, and self-directed learning through experience
- Advocating a balance of reflection and action
- Modeling Heron's extended epistemology and multiple ways of knowing
- Fostering conditions that stimulate the imagination and deal with emotions
- Encouraging playfulness and laughter

- Advocating ongoing assessment and revision of the CI process by group members
- Implementing a systematic plan to transfer responsibility for planning and facilitation to group members

Conclusion

Participants found time in their crowded schedules to learn together through eight cycles of reflection and action, which spiraled through three identifiable phases in the group's learning. In the first phase the group attempted to improve communication and mutual respect by identifying ways to "fix" the staff who reported to them. After engaging in an action in their work units and reflecting on this experience, the nursing managers realized that they needed first to work on communication and mutual respect among themselves. This focus on self became the work of the second learning phase. After growing in their understanding about each other and developing new skills in how they communicated, the nurses entered the third phase of learning. In this third and final learning cycle they used their new skills and capacities to build community throughout the hospital. Marie describes her impression of the CI. "I think that this program helped create more trust for our team. I feel that we're more supportive of each other and we're trying to make each other's jobs more efficient by combining what we can combine. You know we are now thinking of ourselves as one big team or one big hospital—the patient-care thing rather than separate departments."

The decision to initiate a CI often comes from unrest rooted in one's own work experience. Although this CI explored the experience of fragmentation and separation, many topics from practical everyday work experience might be usefully pursued. CI can also be adapted to varying time frames, ranging from weekend retreats for groups and teams to ongoing inquiry sessions.

References

Heron, J. "Helping Whole People Learn." In D. Boud and N. Miller (eds.), *Working with Experience, Animating Learning*. London: Routledge, 1996a.

Heron, J. *Co-operative Inquiry: Research into the Human Condition*. Thousand Oaks, Calif.: Sage, 1996b.

Heron, J. *The Complete Facilitator's Handbook*. London: Kogan Page, 1999.

SUZANNE VAN STRALEN *is an independent consultant specializing in wholistic learning interventions and organizational development. She is also a Ph.D. candidate at the California Institute of Integral Studies in San Francisco. Suzanne can be reached at SVSConsultingServices.com.*

3

Community women learn how to learn from personal experience and use the power of that learning for organizational development. From telling stories and asking questions they also learn how to communicate across complex cultural differences.

Using the Power of Collaborative Inquiry: Community Women Learn and Lead Themselves

Linda L. Smith

Participants: Eleven women, diverse in race, language, and education (ten counselors in an existing community education program on breastfeeding, and the inquiry initiator).

Inquiry purpose: To explore collaborative learning and understand what is needed to expand a small organization devoted to peer education.

Inquiry question: What are the ways we can lower the barriers to peer counseling?

Process: Four-hour meetings at monthly intervals for approximately one year; after the first year, women gradually shifted focus from practice as peer counselors to community outreach and project development. Participants met for two and one-half years.

Outcomes: Participants shifted from being learners who receive knowledge to being learners who construct knowledge. They discovered that cultural difference can be a trusted, creative resource. Using rounds of public discourse, they tested their new knowledge and developed new work.

A few years ago I worked as a collaborative inquirer with a group of diverse community women. For thirty months we used collaborative inquiry to learn together by drawing from our experiences, reflections, and ideas. In the process we also discovered that we, as community women, had acquired particular understanding about how to cross cultural-racial boundaries, a topic of compelling interest to other groups and leaders. Using knowledge of how to nurture cultural difference as a special resource, we expanded our small project by identifying public discourse as a link between collaborative inquiry and organization development. For these reasons the community women's inquiry is a unique case study, using informal learning, extensive diversity, and developmental work activity.

This case is presented from my lens as an adult education researcher and organization development consultant. I was first introduced to collaborative inquiry in 1990 when I discovered theory delineated by Peter Reason (1988) as "new paradigms for human inquiry." What caught my eye immediately was Reason's phrase, "with people" not "on them, for them, or to them." For weeks, I thought about "with people" and imagined what I might do.

How It All Began

In the early 1990s a group of ten community women were awarded a grant to develop peer education services for women who, like themselves, were pregnant or had newborns and wanted to know how to breastfeed. They were led by Ann, the project developer, who was also a breastfeeding mother.

I met the community women when they were just past midway in the two-year grant. All, including Ann, served as volunteers, receiving small stipends for transportation and child care. As part of their project, the women met once a month to pick up materials, submit reports, and talk informally. Together, we decided to do a collaborative inquiry during these monthly sessions, based on the question, *What are the ways we can lower the barriers to peer counseling?* I facilitated the inquiry.

In looking back on the community women's inquiry, I see three important intertwined themes. The first is epistemology. This theme centers on learning to value personal experience as a basis for coming to know. The second theme is cultural difference. It emerged during our work and suggests that collaborative inquiry helps people with diverse backgrounds learn how to communicate across cultural issues that are difficult to talk about. The third theme explores what happens when a CI group communicates its experience through presentations and public discourse. The empowering value of learning through experience aided the community women in seeing the group's knowledge as a small business resource.

In what follows I tell the community women's story three times, tracing their learning through the lens of each theme. I then summarize the women's inquiry with a time line that intertwines the three stories by situating key events chronologically.

First Theme: Adding Knowledge from Experience to Textbook Knowledge Was Like Riding a Seesaw

Most of the literature describing collaborative inquiry appears to presuppose that inquirers have the capacity to think critically and make or construct meaning from their experience (Reason, 1988; Bray, Lee, Smith, and

Yorks, 2000). These capacities imply professional education. In contrast, the community women's education varied from less than high school to university graduate study; most members had completed the equivalent of Grade 12. Our inquiry offers an opportunity to discover what happens in a collaborative group with diverse levels of formal education.

To better understand our collaborative learning, I turned to a model developed by Mary Belenky, Blythe Clinchy, Nancy Goldberger, and Jill Tarule (1986). I believed their work would be useful not only because it was specific to our gender but also because the epistemological phases they describe are especially relevant to understanding women with less formal education. In this model different ways of knowing are identified: silence, knowledge received from others, knowledge derived from the self's subjective perceptions, knowledge derived from procedures, which can be either connected to or separate from self, and finally, knowledge constructed from all these ways of knowing as women develop capacity to construct meaning for themselves.

In reflecting back upon the community women's inquiry, I find that we did move through phases from receiving knowledge to constructing knowledge from our experience. However, our inquiry learning was like riding a seesaw. Our beginning sessions emphasized textbooks as a form of receiving knowledge, with little group attention to using personal experience. Later our learning bounced back and forth between connecting and constructing knowledge like a seesaw moving up and down.

The seesaw bouncing of beliefs and ideas began in the first meeting. The women were committed to promoting practical advice about breastfeeding based on knowledge gained from counselor training and reference books. I was suggesting inquiry, a learning process drawing on experience not found in textbooks. Our effort to communicate about a collaborative inquiry project moved up and down but without a sense of balance.

After that first session the women talked with Ann, who then talked with me. She asked, "What will it take to make collaborative inquiry more concrete? The peer counselors like to work with things they can see." I pondered about what to do. At the next meeting we had a pot luck. In listening to the relaxed way we told recipe stories, I asked us to consider telling stories of what happened between sessions as a way to do the inquiry. The community women agreed.

Later I understood that imagination was a central aspect of learning through collaborative inquiry. Each one of us could tell a story, and through rounds of collaborative storytelling the women had many ways to imagine. Theorists Maxine Greene (1995) and John Heron (1992) write about the importance of imagination in relating experience to knowledge development. Greene says, "It is simply not enough for us to reproduce the way things are. . . . Neither myself, nor my narrative can have, therefore, a single strand. . . . often times the extent to which we grasp another's world depends on our existing ability to make poetic use of our imaginations, to bring in to being 'as if' worlds" (p. 30).

In the third session our stories stressed connecting structures. For instance, Emily closed a counseling story by saying, "This woman is a part of the clinic. It dictates what she can do. We've all been there." This story led to other examples of knowing connected to clinic experience. After telling stories, members of the group referred often to a big book of breast-feeding facts, and we had only glimmers of what counselors thought linked to personal experience.

To stimulate description of personal experience we added tape record-ing to our storytelling. I came to our fourth inquiry meeting with eleven recorders and a stack of audiotapes. "Who wants a recorder?" I asked. Quickly we passed them out. Then we practiced turning the recorders on, saying the wildest words that came to our minds, laughing, and replaying the tapes to hear our voices and laugh some more. Julie, a Latina coun-selor, noted, "I check my English, and it's not all that terrible." Faith observed, "The tapes are much better than writing." Outside our sessions, each member carried her recorder and taped moments she linked to the inquiry.

Soon I had a yearning for other group members to lead us in asking questions, believing that the dynamic of peer questioning would help us learn as a group. I waited and watched for when we were ready. A couple of meetings later, Julie told the story of a young girl who is a new teenage mother living at home. She wants to bottle feed her baby, in order to con-tinue school and a part-time job. Julie brought the story to the group because it was outside the norms of her ethnic community. Then she asked the group, "What advice can you give me?" Eagerly, two women offered solutions. Almost simultaneously, other members of our group began ques-tioning. Once we started asking questions, we did not stop.

Our questions spanned many areas. We asked each other questions about learning through experience and about how we chose the memorable moments that we reported to each other. We asked practical questions, such as, "What are the signs that a woman is ready for peer counseling?" We also asked questions about peer counseling authority outside of breastfeeding education, addressing, for example, what a peer counselor can do in com-municating the need for AIDS screening (Smith, 1995).

As the community women questioned each other more, our ability to construct our own meaning became visible. Rita observed that exploring experience was discovering "the question within the question, with one question leading to another." Through rounds of reflecting on our experi-ences, the community women embraced a particular understanding of peer counseling. We named that learning "mother-to-mother knowledge." Using the model described by Belenky, Clinchy, Goldberger, and Tarule (1986), the naming of mother-to-mother knowledge was a marker of the community women moving from received knowing through connected learning to con-structed meaning in approximately six months of collaborative inquiry.

Second Theme: Crossing Cultures Using Difference as a Trusted, Creative Resource

When I first met the community women I noted that we were like a mini–United Nations; four spoke English as a second language and seven were women of color. Inside our meetings we could immediately see our skin color and hear our language differences. We were also different in relation to our environment. In Washington, D.C., one of the nation's richest regions, we had incomes below the median and we were part-time workers in a location where long work hours are the norm.

Our diversity hung in the air, often visible, but not named. In researching her own life, South African educator Mamphela Ramphele (1995) notes the survival mechanisms that women and people of color throughout the world develop to cope with the difficulties of diversity. She describes the critical challenge of working compassionately and inclusively while also telling the truth about oppression.

After the somewhat unsuccessful first session, Ann suggested that the women have a potluck meal as part of the next meeting. We did, and our foods were from everywhere. We ate Guatemalan tacqueros, West African stew, Caribbean fruit salad, and an Appalachian berry cobbler. In sharing new foods, familiar foods, and some in between, we created an image for helping ourselves to large portions of tasty differences.

While our potluck helped us respect each other, our stories revealed separation based on ethnicity. Latinas paired with Latinas; whites with whites. Emily, who is white, and Rita, who is black, brought insight about the stress of trying to reach across race and culture. Emily said, "I saw the black women waiting for lab work. They looked angry. Their body language says 'Don't talk to me.'" Then Rita quickly commented, "It's like my hesitancy to talk with Hispanic women."

More than sixty years ago anthropologist Ruth Benedict (1934) analyzed patterns across culture. She found that diversity contributes significantly to social creativity and that this phenomenon is true for cultures internally as well as externally. During the seventh month of our inquiry we began to use our differences as a creative resource within our group and describe how to reach across culture outside our group.

Faith told a counseling story. When Faith arrived at the clinic to work as a counselor, the coordinator made it clear that the women spoke only Spanish. Faith is bilingual, but she speaks English and French. Describing to our inquiry group how she talked mostly with her hands and used objects, including a doll, to communicate to the women at the clinic, Faith concluded, "So the trick is to do what it takes to draw them out." When she spoke about gestures, the community women added ways they had learned to cross language barriers. Quickly, we created a list of nonverbal communication tips useful to all.

At the next session the community women returned to talking about crossing culture and race boundaries. Emily and Rita again led the conversation. After telling a story, Emily concluded, "I had a great experience with a black woman. Most of the time that's very hard for me, the body language is usually saying 'Don't approach me.'" With a giggle and delight in her voice Rita asked, "You mean we can be approachable?" Our group laughed, thus indicating a sense of ease and trust with our way of addressing the issue of race (Smith, 1995). We were following a path suggested by education leader Johnetta Cole (1993), who describes true inclusion as being genuinely respectful, with no inferior ways of living, communicating, socializing, or working.

Immediately we took Rita and Emily's discovery into an examination of African American and Hispanic relationships. Early on, Hispanic counselors observed that they assumed most blacks did not want to breastfeed, whereas African American counselors noted that they had thought almost all Hispanics breastfed their babies and knew what to do. Then, with more laughter, we recalled that we had several stories that indicated an opposing truth: blacks had interest in breastfeeding and young Hispanic women wanted alternatives. As we talked, we recognized that our group now had new knowledge about working across culture.

We also saw a special authority from this knowledge of culture and race differences. We defined our learning as "becoming partners," and within our approach we emphasized telling stories, then reflecting, using our stories as touchstones to build trust for working together. In concluding this session, we planned partnership actions for extending the project across our racial and cultural backgrounds: Rita and Emily committed to a series of special raffle and presentation programs; Faith and Julie agreed to work side by side to expand language options; and Ann, Rita and I launched a series of conference and workshop proposals. We believed that we could integrate our new understanding of multicultural inclusion into project plans for advising others. In looking back, Rebecca said, "I think on our meetings as golden. We learned to believe in ourselves, and we all stood taller."

Third Theme: Using Public Discourse to Transfer Knowledge from Our Inquiry to Other Work Projects

As a next step, the community women desired that we take our learning into a broader arena. Practical needs motivated us. In order to continue our reflective work the community women needed money for gas and child care. Both inside and outside our monthly sessions we thought about what we could offer other organizations that would also develop our financial resources.

We knew from observations and experience that organizational leaders were interested in multicultural knowledge. Our understanding of crossing multiple race and cultural boundaries provided us with a particular authority on what it takes to nurture differences as a resource for collaboration. We hoped we might share this knowledge.

Our question—What are the ways we can lower the barriers to peer counseling?—pulled us forward into linking our collaborative inquiry to other organizations and their projects. In pursuing our inquiry about lowering barriers, we identified and tested important reasons for using peer counselors. Implied in our inquiry work was the belief that once they knew more about the value of peer counselors, other groups would want their services.

We turned to the possibility that we might help larger organizations known to fund work. As we had once seen ourselves working "mother-to-mother," we thought we might now work "group-to-group." We observed that community-focused organizations were hiring outreach workers who are like peer counselors. We noted that most of the outreach units or teams had difficulty integrating their work into organizational strategy. With careful thought, we shifted our self-perception to include outreach as a topic about which we felt competent to inquire. We approached leaders of organizations and asked, "What would it take to work better with outreach workers?"

In the group's second year the community women proposed workshops and presentations to build on these hopes and observations. After being accepted we loaded strollers, toddlers, infants, and ourselves into vans, and off we went, talking excitedly. During each presentation we spoke as a unit, with our different voices presenting the whole, or system, of who we were: breastfeeding peer counselors and program outreach workers, community leader-managers with expertise in diversity-based teamwork.

I recognized the value of public discourse from experience with other collaborative inquiry projects (Bray, Lee, Smith, and Yorks, 2000; Zelman, 1995). On our rides home I encouraged the community women to think about audience reactions in order to reflect on our presentations. I asked questions such as, "What happened?" and, "What did we learn that we can use?"

From our public activities the community women quickly developed questions, ideas, and plans for new peer-outreach projects. As a result we nurtured small business activities, constructing links among collaborative inquiry, public discourse, and our organization development. This use of public discourse is consistent with observations about group learning by Elizabeth Kasl and Victoria Marsick (1997). Based on analysis of twenty case studies, these researchers conclude that "going public" accelerates the process of knowledge development for each learning system.

The regional director for the March of Dimes participated in one of the small conferences sponsored by the community women. As was our way, each of us had a particular role in presenting our stories and facilitating storytelling among the wider group to help all explore community project development. Immediately afterward the director wanted to know more. A few weeks later we agreed to undertake a program inquiry sponsored by the

March of Dimes, which engaged leaders of thirty-two nonprofit organizations. Once again the inquiry meetings were like a mini–United Nations— smiling, earnest faces; important stories from diverse experiences and questions from diverse perspectives, all available for inquirers to gather and transform into knowledge.

Inquiry Time Line

In Exhibit 3.1 I have arranged the key events from the three themes into one chronological account of the inquiry.

Exhibit 3.1. Chronological Overview of Inquiry

Before the inquiry: Breastfeeding project funded to provide volunteer peer education.

Month 1: First inquiry session; highly diverse grassroots group members assume that needed knowledge is in textbooks.

Month 2: Potluck dinner; diversity is visible, unnamed. We decide inquiry question, "What are the ways we can lower barriers to peer counseling?"

Month 3: Incorporate storytelling.

Month 4: Add audio taping to assist storytelling. When Emily describes racial boundaries, women do not respond or ask questions.

Month 7: Faith tells clinic story of crossing language and cultural barriers. Julie leads women in asking questions. We decide peer counseling is "mother-to-mother" education and learning from personal experience is key.

Month 8: Emily and Rita lead group in crossing race and cultural difference to become authentically inclusive. Rebecca observes that we are all standing taller in our learning. We create new projects led by diverse partners and name our plans "becoming partners."

Months 10–15: We observe that peer counselors are similar to outreach workers in other agencies. Plan presentations.

Month 12: Public funding ends. Begin workshops and conference presentations as a form of public discourse.

Month 17: Host community workshop; March of Dimes regional director participates.

Month 20: Proposal to March of Dimes for regional inquiry with use of community women as facilitators and presenters.

Months 18–24: Continue with presentations and workshops.

Months 25–28: Host regional collaborative inquiry workshops.

Months 28–29: Analyze findings from regional inquiries.

Month 30: Meet for the last time as large group; members make commitment to continue helping each other.

An Invitation to Collaborative Inquiry and Public Discourse: Making Work Knowledge More Accessible

As an adult learning professional who consults on projects in education, health care, and hospitality-tourism sectors, I believe that collaborative inquiry offers hope for these work settings. Like the community women's project, these workplaces abound with worker experiences that can be transformed into new knowledge. And like the community women, customer- and direct-service workers in these sectors experience the unexpected and work with many differences to meet customer expectations. Creative managers are seeking knowledge about context-centered services. More can be done to help staff development for changing work tasks by using collaborative inquiry coupled with public discourse. Inquiry helps learners tap experiences for practical knowledge that is tailored and tested by the group reflection process. When public discourse is added, learning is pooled, thus becoming a reservoir. Creative managers and workers alike can access this inquiry-driven knowledge reservoir for innovation.

The community women's inquiry is the story of tapping a work knowledge reservoir. By inquiring collaboratively into personal experience we expanded our knowledge and sense of personal authority. Through multiple presentations and workshops we used public discourse to accelerate what we knew and build our credentials. Along the way of that discourse we also constructed opportunities for new business projects. Our story is an invitation to all who have a yearning to use knowledge from a collaborative experience and apply that learning to new work projects.

References

Belenky, M., Clinchy, B., Goldberger, N., and Tarule, J. *Women's Ways of Knowing.* New York: Basic Books, 1986.

Benedict, R. *Patterns of Culture.* Boston, Mass.: Houghton-Mifflin, 1934.

Bray, J. N., Lee, J., Smith, L. L., and Yorks, L. *Collaborative Inquiry in Practice: Action, Reflection, and Making Meaning.* Thousand Oaks, Calif.: Sage, 2000.

Cole, J. *Straight Talk with America's Sister President.* New York: Doubleday, 1993.

Greene, M. *Releasing the Imagination.* San Francisco: Jossey-Bass, 1995.

Heron, J., *Feeling and Personhood: Psychology in Another Key.* Thousand Oaks, Calif.: Sage, 1992.

Kasl, E., and Marsick, V. "Epistemology of Groups as Learning Systems: A Research-Based Analysis." *Crossing Borders, Breaking Boundaries, Research in the Education of Adults, An International Conference: Proceedings of the 27th Annual Conference of the Standing Conference on University Teaching and Research in the Education of Adults (SCUTREA).* London: Birbeck College, University of London, 1997.

Ramphele, M. *A Life.* Cape Town, South Africa: David Philip Publishers, 1995.

Reason, P. (ed.). *Human Inquiry in Action: Developments in New Paradigm Research.* Newbury Park, Calif.: Sage, 1988.

Smith, L. L. "Collaborative Inquiry as an Adult Learning Strategy." *Dissertation Abstracts International* 56 (7), 2533. University Microfilms no. AAC95–39867, 1995.

Zelman, A. W. "Answering the Question: 'How Is Learning Experienced in Collaborative Inquiry?' A Phenomenological/Hermeneutic Approach." *Dissertation Abstracts International*, 56 (7), 2534. University Microfilms no. AAC95–39885, 1995.

LINDA L. SMITH uses storytelling and group inquiry to help workplaces work better. Living in Washington, D.C., she leads a consulting practice that emphasizes work culture, creativity, and team performance and frequently serves as faculty to Georgetown and George Washington Universities.

4

The collaborative inquiry group on intuition met in a college setting to discuss what participants had acknowledged internally but not discussed openly. They validated intuition as a way of knowing and learned how to nurture it in themselves and others.

Nurturing Intuition Through Group Learning

Annette Weinberg Zelman

Participants: Seven inquirers—six women and one man. Five are faculty and two are administrators at a community college in New York State. Five are in the humanities and two are in the sciences.

Inquiry purpose: To explore the role of intuition in an educational setting; to nurture intuition among ourselves and in our students.

Inquiry question: How can we promote or nurture intuition?

Process: Six sessions over eight months. Action and reflection were incorporated into inquiry sessions.

Outcomes: Participants validated intuition as a way of knowing and gained confidence through discussing intuition openly. Inquiry was viewed as "an open process" and a kind of "performance art."

I have always been an intuitive person, relying upon nonverbal signals or subconscious modes of awareness to evaluate people and situations. When I broached the idea of an inquiry on intuition with colleagues at the community college where I served as an administrator, I was greeted with either bemusement or an apparent glazing over of the eyes. Ultimately, I found five faculty members who asked whether they might become participants in the inquiry or who responded "yes" when I asked directly if they would join. All but one of the participants identified themselves as being intuitive, and all acknowledged having been reluctant to discuss intuition with others.

Initiating

The group's formation extended over a period of several months. I held a number of preliminary discussions with interested individuals, asking each to suggest prospective participants. Those who responded positively were in the fields of literature, art history, communications, and nursing. In an effort to bring another perspective to the group, I invited a professor of psychology to join; she agreed.

I stayed in touch with those who were committed to joining the endeavor by sending a letter in which I suggested readings about the topics of collaborative inquiry and intuition. I made clear that these were merely suggestions, that no reading was required at any time during the collaborative inquiry process. The letter also related the role the inquiry on intuition would play in my doctoral work. I assured participants, "The inquiry group is an autonomous entity with its own rules and parameters, functioning as an independent association of peers. The goal is to create knowledge within the group and to observe the process" (Zelman, 1995, p. 353).

Convening

During the morning of the first session, anxious to begin the inquiry, I forgot to have people introduce themselves. I began by describing criteria for collaborative inquiry and suggested that the group might change them. Anticipating discussion on each criterion, I felt surprised when the group expressed very little interest in the strategy as such.

The first meeting consisted of morning and afternoon sessions, with lunch served between. A relaxed atmosphere contributed to revelations through storytelling, which in turn contributed to immediate intimacy and trust. The group pounced on the topic of intuition as if there were no time to be wasted in extraneous issues—including belaboring collaborative inquiry. Committed to learning about intuition but not to the process of inquiry, the group felt free to experiment with the form.

I was concerned about the criterion of "level playing field," since I was an administrator and most members of the group were faculty. Prior to our first session I had asked each prospective participant whether he or she would feel self-conscious about possible conflicts between faculty and administrators. None seemed to care about the issue. It was I who needed reassurance that the difference in our positions would not create a serious impediment to the work of the group.

During our first session, confidentiality surfaced as a group concern. We agreed that "what's said here isn't talked about outside." Because of my dissertation work, the group permitted me to audiotape our meetings, and I promised to have the tapes transcribed outside the county to safeguard the participants' privacy.

The group coalesced immediately through members' avid interest in intuition and delight in finding colleagues with whom the topic might be discussed. Sensing a consensual understanding, we did not require a verbal definition for what we knew to be nonverbal. Attempts at this session and later sessions to define intuition met with silence or mild but firm resistance.

The venue of our early meetings contributed to the group's closeness. The first four meetings were in a small, isolated classroom in the second sublevel of the college library. Most of us had never seen the room before and had no associations with it. A square table filled most of the space; we sat around the table—two, two, two, and one. There was a blackboard, which the group never used, gray carpet on the floor, a low hum from the air-conditioning system, one door that led to the hallway, and no windows. Ruth referred to the space as "another universe." It was here that we formed our trust and our mode of operating.

For our fifth meeting we moved to a new location: the television studio, which is two stories high and very spacious. Painted black, the room contains scaffolding, television cameras, screens, and stored furniture used in production work. There are no windows to the outside. Through an internal window, we could see television production equipment, as well as students and faculty; they paid no attention to us and we did not respond to their presence. In the middle of this space is a raised dais where we sat in comfortable armchairs around a circular antique oak table. All future meetings were held here. In this grand space our activities took on a new dimension, becoming freer and soaring into new realms. In subsequent sessions, we considered "sense of place" and listened to music.

Acting and Reflecting

In drawing the group together, I suggested a possible inquiry question, "How is intuition used in teaching and learning?" and a recommended alternative, "Can we promote intuition in ourselves and others?" Wording the question took second place to exploring the topic. Eventually, after several sessions, the question evolved into, "How can we promote or nurture intuition?" Participants discovered that they felt intuition in the classroom was of secondary importance; primary interest lay in nurturing and promoting intuition in ourselves.

We tackled the challenge of designing actions that could help us answer our question. The concept of action outside the group and reflection within the group did not appeal to participants. Intuition, we agreed, does not surface on demand; thus, it would be impossible to give ourselves action assignments that call forth intuition. We settled on a format of bringing exercises to the group and reflecting on them immediately.

The group dismissed suggestions for exercises of a physical nature. Each exercise was done as we sat at a table. I introduced the first exercise, which required that each person make lists of associations. Other exercises included writing freely and reading to the group. These exercises caused great discomfort. Members described a sense of being tested; some expressed feeling that there might be right and wrong answers.

Despite the discomfort caused by these exercises, there were lessons learned. We compared intuition with the creative process and identified fear, discomfort, and self-consciousness as impediments to creativity.

Designing the Process

Leah suggested that we try exercises "without a conclusion" and volunteered to provide one at the next session. At that session she brought in five poster-size reproductions of paintings: one by Matisse, one by Magritte, and others by less well-known artists. The discussion that ensued was free-flowing and touched on some of our experiences with students in the classroom.

Leah's exercise did not engender the discomfort we experienced during the previous session. The earlier exercises, introduced by three participants, had all required word associations and writing exercises that required personal disclosures. Leah's exercise was oral, requiring reactions based on visual presentations. The earlier exercises felt like tests; they were done on paper, a medium associated with academic testing. We felt safer to disclose ideas that were once removed—based on an intermediary media, the artwork, rather than directly from our internal thoughts. We did not consciously choose one kind of exercise over others; an intuitive process led us to accept Leah's approach as less threatening. Subsequent presenters adopted the less-threatening format.

The exercises at most of our sessions were the "action" portion of an action-reflection cycle. Claire described our discussions as both action and reflection: "Our statements or interactions were nearly always self-conscious and self-reflective." At the end of each session, we processed what had occurred during the session but made little attempt to bring ourselves back to the inquiry question or reflect on collaborative inquiry as such.

Learning took place primarily through an accretion of anecdotes, thus building layers of shared experience. Important elements include increased awareness of intuitive incidents in everyday experience, willingness to call attention to intuitive experiences in everyday situations, a series of exercises that helped the group stimulate and reflect on intuition, and reports by individuals on their intuitive experiences, many related to teaching and learning in the classroom.

Encountering

Victoria reflected that there was nothing she particularly wanted from the sessions. "I'm perfectly happy." Looking at me, she continued, "I could start worrying: 'Are you getting what you need and want out of this?'" I assured the group that there was nothing to worry about and countered with my concern that the group not "feel that you're trying to do a job for me." In a later session, my fears were somewhat allayed when Victoria said, "I've stopped worrying about what you need for your dissertation and interestingly enough. . . . how could I possibly know what you need?"

Victoria suggested that the conversation had been a "study in intuitive leaps that people make." In this context, she said, "I feel both understood and understanding."

Referring to the freedom to speak openly, William said, "I sense a wonderful sense of nonjudgmental tone in everything that's happened since day one. . . . There's been a very careful listening that we just have fallen into that I find is relatively unusual." Victoria commented, "It's the quality of not having a specific agenda that allows people to really listen and hear and respond and also allows this sort of spiral to happen."

One exercise consisted of viewing a video produced by William, entitled, "Aspects of the Arts: A Sense of Place." In the discussion that ensued, Ruth suggested that to nurture intuition there had to be a "sense of not knowing all the answers." Claire suggested that intuition generated a sense of "timelessness" in which people did not "hoard" or weigh their energies but were "open to process." The same might be said of the collaborative inquiry process as it was unfolding in this group.

At our sixth session, Claire introduced a Brahms violin concerto. She then showed a short portion of the film "Defending Your Life" to illustrate the theme of fear as an impediment to intuition. At this session we again returned to our personal experiences with intuition. We were acknowledging and "nurturing" our own intuition, validating it, and giving ourselves permission to recognize and support it in others.

Making Sense

Each of our six inquiry sessions was devoted almost exclusively to intuition. After I introduced collaborative inquiry in our first session, the topic was not raised again until our focus session, held a month after our last intuition discussion. The group had agreed to conduct a faculty development workshop. Surprising to me at the time, the group chose collaborative inquiry as its topic for the workshop, not intuition. In retrospect I believe that the group, having experienced collaborative inquiry, felt comfortable in commenting on it as an instrument for creating meaning that could have value for other educators. More important, although we felt totally free to discuss intuition among ourselves, we were not yet comfortable with the topic among "nonbelievers."

The collaborative inquiry on intuition was a somewhat atypical experience in that there was a fluid and porous relationship between action and reflection, with action-reflection being experienced simultaneously. In addition, participants did not articulate an inquiry question early in the process, nor did they feel it necessary to define their topic, that is, to define intuition.

The group on intuition had a primary motivation that did not require an introduction. Participants were passionately interested in the topic for personal reasons. Although some in the group expressed later that they had wanted to help me with my studies, this concern was secondary to interest in intuition. This project provided a first opportunity to explore a way of knowing that all had experienced but had been uncomfortable acknowledging to others.

What some in the group treasured most was that there was no pre-scribed roadmap for making the journey. Claire suggested that if she already knew where she was going, she would not bother making the trip. This was not a group with an agenda, a determined path, or a destination. We experienced our discussions as a "luxury" because no immediate product was required. The sessions were marked by "swirls," silences, meanderings, or "hope-filled detouring that happens when you allow yourself to go 'off' on a tangent." The group welcomed having the topic determine the flow of the discussions.

Facilitating

As the initiator, and somewhat in the "directorial" position, as William described it, I might have been more directive. Initially I played my role as "director" passively. I had experienced, throughout my life, situations in the academic and political spheres in which leaders solicited discussion only as a stratagem to convey democratic participation; in reality, the opinions of the leader dominated. This was not always due solely to the leader's short-comings; often the group was complicit. I was determined not to manipulate others. I was also concerned about my supervisory capacity as an administrator and did not want this status to carry weight in the inquiry.

The group did not follow suggestions that I made when my suggestions were counter to members' desires. Two examples come to mind. When I initiated the group, I brought a set of criteria for governing the collaborative inquiry process, explaining that we might change the criteria if we wanted. Not until the formal inquiry was over did the group show any interest in examining the criteria. As we prepared for the faculty development workshop, participants suggested some changes. Although I tried several times to have intuition defined and to have the inquiry question refined, this was not what the group wanted. In "hearing" the silences and the resistances, I felt that I was engaging in the intuitive process I had known in my teaching. In letting the process happen I placed my trust in the group participants and process and was rewarded by earning the group's trust.

In the beginning, I agonized over my role. Before the group convened, I wrote, "My fear is that my need for closure, part of my learning style, will put me in the role of facilitator." When I raised the issue of rotating the role of facilitator, the group rejected the suggestion. But by taking on the rotation of exercises, the group had tacitly agreed to alternate facilitators.

I continued to worry: Was I being too directive? Not directive enough? Was I holding back so as not to skew the discussion or was I contributing too much in an effort to move the discussions along? In either case, was I being true to myself and to the group? I often held back, fearing I would promote my ideas too forcefully. William Torbert helped me understand how to participate authentically. When I brought up my concern in a small seminar, he suggested, "All you're modeling is powerlessness if you don't intervene." His observation gave me "permission" to contribute more freely. I felt more at ease when a thought came to mind. Ruth later said that my "sense of conflict was not particularly evident."

While I was struggling with my role, others were quite comfortable. Claire reflected, "The moment and the materials create something. And it's no more me, or my ego connected to it." The process developed into an easy exchange of ideas. There was always careful consideration of what others were saying without attempts to be argumentative or "right." Group members expressed their ideas without attempting to convince others.

Acknowledging

In using the collaborative inquiry process, the group became adept in that process. Rupert Sheldrake (1988), in *The Presence of the Past: Morphic Resonance and the Habits of Nature*, explores the possibility that "memory is inherent in nature" and that "all humans draw upon a collective memory, to which all in turn contribute" (p. xvii). Sheldrake suggests that there is a "formative causation" in which there is a "progressive establishment of new habits" (p. xviii). The group on intuition, by accepting the model of collaborative inquiry and learning through that mode, experienced collaborative inquiry, though the group was not consciously devoted to the learning cycle or the specific criteria. In using this mode of inquiry, the group became proficient at it and was able to contribute to the store of knowledge about collaborative inquiry without prolonged discussions about how they experienced the model. Although group members might have spent more time before making final commitments to work together, it is unlikely that there would have been a beneficial effect in belaboring the topic of collaborative inquiry. Experience was the great educator.

The group had designed its own process—perhaps intuitively. Having experienced collaborative inquiry, the group was able to describe it for others, in this case, at a workshop it organized for faculty colleagues. Members demonstrated that they owned collaborative inquiry in a fresh—and conscious—way. For example, in reviewing the criteria for collaborative inquiry, members drew on their experience in order to make suggestions for changes.

Concluding

The intuition inquiry group's findings on collaborative inquiry contributed significantly to my dissertation work in which themes surfaced:

Theme 1: Learning Is Experienced as a Striving for Equilibrium Between the Individual and the Group. Claire, a published poet, described what happens through the collaborative process as giving up ego in the group: "I definitely feel that there's a shared venture, shared sense of investigation." She compared the process to a "poem process, or with any kind of writing, or any creative activity, where the moment and the materials create something. And it's no more me, or my ego connected to it. And I think of the inquiry process as being this sort of construct that isn't really me, individually. I'm an element in it."

Theme 2: Learning Is Experienced as Enhanced Access to Nonlinguistic Knowing. There are three indicators that learning is experienced as enhanced access to nonverbal knowing. The first is the obvious one of the group being conscious of intuitive knowing and conscious of how being in the group allowed us to acknowledge this knowing.

The second indicator is the way the group used collaborative inquiry for six sessions without accepting it consciously. Only later did collaborative inquiry became a recognized part of the group's thinking.

A third example of access to nonlinguistic knowing is illuminated by Victoria. She noticed that we often made hand gestures to illustrate an idea. She said that it was obvious to her that we "knew," and our bodies expressed our knowledge before we were able to verbalize. Intuition or nonverbal knowing preceded linguistic knowing.

Theme 3: Learning Is Experienced as an Empowering Process. What was important to participants in the inquiry was that in permitting ourselves to examine intuition we were validating it as a way of knowing. Grace was grateful for the "greater confidence" in our "own intuitive inner voice" so that we did not have "to discount this" as being "wrong." She observed that once a person can accept this way of knowing with confidence, "then the fear goes away and you can be intuitive and access your creative self." Several people spoke about the group's strongly expressed affirmation of a way of knowing, previously held secret. Feeling supported, some were more confident expressing their intuitive knowledge outside the group.

Theme 4: Learning Is Experienced as Energizing. Although the process of collaborative inquiry was viewed as "not time effective," what it generates in releasing creative energies is deemed a compensatory factor. William suggested the process was like a "jazz group" performing variations on a theme. The creative process gave energy to what we did.

Theme 5: Learning Is Experienced as a Change in Critical Subjectivity and Critical Intersubjectivity. This theme is related to the giving up of "ego" in the group and in feeling assuredness in our way of knowing outside the group. As a direct result of the learning that occurred through the process, some participants were able to take risks in the "outside" world they would not have considered possible prior to this experience.

Theme 6: Learning Is Experienced as Having a "Boundary-less" Quality. The group felt free to roam in our discussions, comparing the process to having a good conversation with a friend. Victoria commented on several occasions that there was "no container" in the process.

We noted that participants needed to have confidence in one another and that the process itself was productive. Collaborative inquiry required an investment in time and the ability to allow for the emergent nature of the learning. Since there was no preconceived product, we were free to wander in any direction we chose; having a product changes the direction of the discussions. Since none in the group felt an individual ownership of the knowledge that emerged, all were responsible for propelling the process and the learning.

References

Sheldrake, R. *The Presence of the Past: Morphic Resonance and the Habits of Nature.* New York: Vintage Books, 1988.

Zelman, A. "Answering the Question, 'How Is Learning Experienced in Collaborative Inquiry?': A Phenomenological/Hermeneutic Approach." *Dissertation Abstracts International,* 56 (7), 2534. University Microfilms No. AAC95–39885, 1995.

ANNETTE WEINBERG ZELMAN *is executive director of Cornell Cooperative Extension in Westchester County, New York. She has been an educator and administrator in academic institutions in the Lower Hudson Valley.*

5

Working within a liberal feminist Christian tradition, six women seek to nurture learning communities that empower and transform. Metaphor and laughter guide their way in realizing Spirit is their Co-inquirer.

Midwife to a Learning Community: Spirit as Co-inquirer

Whitney Wherrett Roberson

Participants: Four professional women, joined two years into the inquiry by two new participants. All are European American, middle-class, middle-aged.

Initiator's purpose: To explore ways of empowering transformative learning and to experience collaborative inquiry as an adult education strategy.

Inquiry question: From the abundance of my heart, soul, mind, and body, how can I contribute to the conception and nurture of learning communities that empower and transform?

Process: Six-hour meetings at monthly intervals for one year, then three-hour monthly meetings. The group has met for five years.

Outcomes: Participants became more aware of themselves and others as choice-makers and of themselves as agents of transformation. They identified and practiced processes that facilitate transformation, especially deep listening, storytelling, being present to others as companions on the journey, and being open to the presence of creative Spirit.

"When I arrived, my daughter was terribly weary; she was fully dilated but nothing much seemed to be happening. We were all feeling discouraged when the labor nurse dropped by, took in the situation and said in a calm, firm voice: 'You've got to *talk* to this baby.' And that's just what we started

---

This chapter was written in collaboration with Devena D. Reed, Deborah Gavrin Frangquist, Bavi Rivera, Mary S. Kimball, and Mary Hill Atwood.

to do. Gently, soothingly at first, we encouraged the baby to come and he did, actually turning himself around! Believe me, by the time he started down the birth canal, we were cheering him on for all we were worth!'"

Birth of a Question

Just telling the story, Devena lit up with enthusiasm, and so did the rest of us. "That's it!" we found ourselves exclaiming, "That's our question: 'How do we talk to the baby?!'" For some hours our fledgling collaborative inquiry group had been struggling to formulate an inquiry question that would capture our passion for discovering ways to facilitate growth and transformation within the various communities in which we lived and worked. In telling the story of her grandson's birth, one of us had found the metaphor that seemed to capture our desire perfectly. Indeed, her story seemed to effect in us what it was describing, for within a few minutes we brought forth—gave birth to—our inquiry question: "From the abundance of my heart, soul, mind, and body, how can I contribute to the conception and nurture of learning communities that empower and transform?"

Inquiry Energized by Spirit

Even at this first "official" session of our collaborative inquiry group, we had begun to experience what we would later recognize as the presence of Spirit in our inquiry process: there was something almost palpable about the energy of the group. Although we'd been meeting almost five hours none of us were exhausted. Quite the contrary, we were more energized when we finished the day than when we'd begun; for each of us, our time together had been life-giving rather than life-draining. We were excited about our question, about what we'd already begun to learn, and about the action steps we'd generated. Elizabeth Kasl, who mentored our group in the early phase of our inquiry, dropped in on us at one point during the day and, sensing this energy, shared with us Peter Reason's observation that "co-operative inquiry is out of control." She went on to explain that co-operative or collaborative inquiry "takes on such a vital life of its own, it just sweeps you along with it."

"That sounds like the Holy Spirit to me," quipped one of us, and we all laughed in recognition.

We were, after all, four women not unacquainted with matters of spirit. We were all liberal, feminist Christians: two of us, Whitney and Devena, were Episcopal seminarians, Nedi was an Episcopal priest and rector of a parish, and Deborah was an active member of that same parish. What had brought us together on this occasion, however, was not our faith but a passionate desire to find new ways of learning and sharing knowledge, new ways of deepening self-understanding in ourselves and others, new ways of empowering and transforming. We had met briefly for the first time four weeks earlier in response to Whitney, a seminary student eager to experiment with innovative learning strategies, who had determined to try collaborative inquiry. A handful of interested participants seemed to materialize as if on cue: a chance conversation here, a phone call there, and the group was networked into existence.

We expected collaborative inquiry to offer both a context and a strategy for exploring transformative learning. We didn't anticipate that the methodology itself would not only accommodate the spiritual dimension of our learning but actually open us more fully to it. As we later came to recognize, it was as if Spirit became our Co-inquirer.

We find it somewhat difficult to conceptualize what we mean by *Spirit* or *Holy Spirit*. We situate ourselves within a tradition, Christianity, which has carried on a lively conversation—even debate—for almost two thousand years about the nature of divine Mystery, including the meaning of Holy Spirit. We live in a time when our own culture seems open to the possibility that the spiritual dimension is real and the basis for a deeper wholeness. And yet significant factors inhibit public discourse about matters spiritual. Our culture seems to lack both a common vocabulary with which to discuss spiritual Reality and adequate contexts in which an open dialogue can occur.

Readers within our tradition might understand theological language were we to use it; however, we suspect that what we've experienced in our learning community is not just a "Christian thing" but a Reality present in most collaborative inquiries, though perhaps not always named. We want to point to this possibility. But how to speak of it? Words such as *transpersonal* and *Higher Power* are sometimes heard in nontheological circles, although they're not ones with which we're particularly conversant. Peter Reason (1993) speaks of "sacred inquiry" and John Heron (1998, 2001) of "sacred science" and "spiritual inquiry," but we are not entirely certain such terms encompass our experience. Perhaps it makes the most sense simply to describe the phenomenon as we have experienced and conceptualized it for ourselves and invite you the reader to look for the parallels in your own experience, naming these in whatever ways seem appropriate and comfortable.

Metaphor as Mediator of Spirit and Meaning

One of the first places we noticed the presence or release of spiritual energy was when a powerful image was generated within the group. The paragraphs that begin this chapter bear witness to this phenomenon. Devena's story of giving birth and "midwiving" actually continued an image that had presented itself at a brief exploratory meeting before any of us had committed to the inquiry itself. On this occasion we noted that the metaphor of "midwifery" seemed to capture our passion to assist in the birthing of something new, yet already present, within ourselves and others. We realized what we wanted was to be "midwives-in-training." Naming ourselves as "Midwives" gave us a sense of identity and also signified our commitment to one another and the inquiry process. The metaphor itself seemed to draw us together, helping form us into a learning community. Its discovery released excitement in and among us, a vital energy that we've come to associate with the presence of Spirit.

Although we didn't recognize it clearly at the time, the discovery of this central, defining metaphor was a spiritual experience. It carried us deeper into our own wisdom, becoming a kind of door through which we could enter into meaning. For example, the images clustered around midwiving and birth-giving reassured us during that first six-hour meeting when the movement toward articulating our question seemed painfully slow and meandering. "Birth is messy," remarked one of us, "but you don't think about that while it's happening." We laughed, and the insight was immediately taken up by Nedi, the parish priest, who related it to a situation in her parish that seemed "chaotic" to some parishioners but that she recognized intuitively as creative. Perhaps a certain amount of creative chaos is part of transformative learning, we mused, already beginning to answer the inquiry question we were still laboring to formulate. As though confirming our own insight—that chaos can be a creative step on the way to articulation—we moved almost immediately to hearing Devena's story and "birthing" our inquiry question.

More birth stories followed as the group took the image and the meaning deeper. Deborah, then a college administrator, told of her own difficult labor and delivery, describing how the group of doctors, nurses, and interns who had gathered to witness a breach birth became—almost in spite of themselves—a community of support for her. "What I felt," she said, "was that they were all on my side." Then immediately making the application to our inquiry question, she added, "We're talking about creating the kind of environment where everybody knows what's meant and needed and does it."

Nedi took the thought farther: "So it's not just talking to the baby; it's talking to the birth-givers."

Devena, one of the seminarians, laughingly recalled the metaphor of "Mother Church" which Deborah expanded: "It's not just one baby."

"Or," added Whitney, "one birth-giver. Hey! It's a collaborative labor!" The group exploded with laughter as we found the images of our own experience as women suddenly enlivened with fresh meaning, the images at once validated by and validating of the inquiry process.

Metaphors often pointed to aspects of our experience that we might not have noticed otherwise: for example, the waiting and attending involved in pregnancy and birth-giving made us aware of the role waiting plays in empowering others. We could apply that insight. Our action steps often involved waiting and watching to see what was happening in the organizations in which we were living and working. Metaphor seemed to provide a sort of "meaning bridge," permitting us to cross from experience to conceptualization and thence to concrete action.

Even in the first meetings of our learning community we were discovering what we already knew, making meaning of our experience and seeing new contexts for applying this meaning. Metaphor had carried us there, and behind or in the metaphor, we were beginning to realize, was a dynamic, vital energy: Spirit. We experienced our metaphors as inSpired.

Laughter as a Sign of Spirit

Laughter often seemed to accompany our metaphor-borne insights; a wonderful energy was liberated when we happened upon just the right image to connect experience with new or unexpected meaning. At our second meeting, Deborah was reflecting on the fact that between our meetings she had discovered that the *action* and the *reflection* of the inquiry were happening for her virtually on top of one another. She likened it to a sonic boom, telling us about how her son had explained this phenomenon to his younger sister: "He told her to think of all the sound that happens as an ordinary plane approaches, then is overhead, and then is gone. And then think about what would happen if all that sound were added together and there was no warning and suddenly it was there and then it was over."

Nedi agreed, laughing that the inquiry process had affected every other meeting in her life until she'd lost track of where she'd gotten insights. Yes! We all joined her laughter, recognizing the phenomenon.

Later in the conversation we returned to this experience of applying our reflective insights. Generating a new image—"It's like gardening, where you plow some of the crop right back into the soil [to enrich it]."—we laughed as we realized we had made immediate use of the insights in an entirely new way. Once again, image bridged experience with meaning-making, releasing lively energy. This joyful energy, too, we experienced as Spirit, and from our own faith tradition remembered that joy has always been seen as a gift and sign of holy Spirit.

Our laughter began to create in us another effect often associated with Spirit: the building of intimate, trust-filled community. None of us had known the others well—or at all—before the initiation of our inquiry. Yet before very long we found ourselves making meaning together from our life challenges and the deepest musings of our hearts. It was as though the laughter opened us, gracefully making us vulnerable to one another, readying us to hear one another deeply and preparing us for the sometimes unsettling experience of being heard.

In the first months of the inquiry, each of us was, in her own life context, dealing with significant vocational issues or transitions. Nedi had just assumed the pastoral leadership of her parish. Deborah was dealing with a demanding job that, unbeknownst to her, she was about to leave. Whitney and Devena were both experiencing obstacles in their ordination process. Yes, we wanted to be "midwives" to others, but we found ourselves also wanting and needing a womb of our own (!), a protective community in which we could make sense of the change and growth occurring in our own lives. At one of our early meetings, Deborah read an excerpt from a book by Nelle Morton (1986, pp. 127–129) in which Morton describes a community of women who "heard one another into speech." This capacity described exactly the sort of community we were becoming and that we wanted to help create. Again, we experienced our opening to one another with growing trust and mutual vulnerability as divine Hospitality, facilitated by the presence of Spirit in our midst.

Spirit in Action and Conflict

It was not always a comfortable process, and indeed, at one point we reminded ourselves that there are times when a protective environment can become dysfunctional. If our collaborative inquiry community were to be more than a simple support group, its "cervix" must eventually open and the "baby" be pushed into the world. Our work together must somehow effect real change, our action steps result in transformation. Even when the transformation was unpleasant, we experienced—sometimes retrospectively and sometimes in the moment—the presence of Spirit.

At one point, for example, we found ourselves talking about "hegemonic discourse" and its power to oppress and disempower. As we searched our own experience for ways that we "marked" others and were ourselves "marked," Deborah began to realize that her professional dress "marked" her within the academic institution where she worked. Her action step as a result of our reflection was to pay closer attention to this marking, asking how her clothes either marked or left her unmarked in relation to the various groups with which she interacted professionally. Deborah's noticing eventually led her to the conclusion that her institutional environment was not one in which she could do the empowering and nurturing work to which she was drawn. She left her job to start a business in which she could live out her call to be an agent of transformation.

Recalling the experience later, Deborah reflected with gratitude on the "persistent presence of the Spirit with me" mediated through the Midwives' inquiry process. "I [now] experience that very difficult time as one of being led, kicking and screaming, out of captivity in a small space into new life— [of] being born again."

Community as Container for InSpired Action

Perhaps one of our most powerful experiences of Spirit-in-action was an occasion of significant conflict in which the group itself became the crucible containing the transformative action. It occurred over a period of weeks at an odd time in the life of our inquiry. After we had been meeting for several years, the four of us decided to invite two other women to join us. Once again, it was a period of significant transition for three of the original four. Deborah was starting her new business. Devena and Whitney had both graduated from seminary: Whitney was working in a parish, and Devena, stalled in her ordination process, had returned to her work with the state department of education.

Devena had been unable to attend the meetings for a number of months, and about the time she rejoined the group Whitney's attendance became sporadic. As it happened, Whitney and Devena were almost never at the same meeting. The reconstituted group had made several attempts to formulate a new inquiry question, but perhaps because attendance of the group was unstable, these attempts had faltered. When all six women were finally able to meet together, a number of significant changes had occurred: Whitney had been ordained, Devena had returned to the group in Whitney's absence, and the newcomers were now regular members.

When a work-related situation prevented Whitney from attending yet another meeting, Devena sent Whitney a "confrontational" e-mail, intended to share her experience of Whitney and offer feedback about her participation in the group. The e-mail puzzled and angered Whitney, and the two began a correspondence of some weeks in which they tried to hear one another—without success. Each woman now tells the story in her own words:

Devena's Story

After Whit didn't show up at that last meeting, I announced to the group that Whit's absence really bothered me. I was seriously considering whether to separate from the group myself. This brought up many conflicts for me. One was that the Midwives group was a vestige of my seminary experience. With my ordination blocked I was tempted to compare myself to Cinderella's stepsister.

The e-mailed discussion brought about by my confrontation of Whitney was not very satisfactory. I tried to own my own confusing emotions [and] to keep my comments about her behavior descriptive and nonjudgmental. However, when I experienced Whitney's comments as implying that something was wrong with me psychologically for bringing about such a confrontation, I sent a concluding message.

Whitney Continues

Devena's experience of me was very different from my experience of myself, and I felt hurt, confused, and then angry. I didn't know what was going on. I was never more tempted simply to withdraw.

Yet this is where Spirit comes in again, for it then occurred to me that it would be supremely ironic if a group called into being around the question of creating transforming learning communities failed to become one itself when the going got rough. We'd been "talking the talk"—trying to make real meaning of our experience—but could we now "walk the talk" to let that meaning transform our *own* life together? Something in me wanted to be faithful to the spirit of our inquiry, and I knew I couldn't be faithful without hanging in there to see what new thing might emerge. I suggested to Devena the possibility of asking the other Midwives to help us "hold" our conversation, realizing I'd have to choose vulnerability, trusting there was indeed Something Greater involved in our process.

Devena Continues

> I too sensed the presence of Spirit in this. I wrote [to Whit] "I do want a safe container for growing for myself as well as you. I understood as I approached you. . . . that dialogue would require a willingness from both of us to be vulnerable. I trust you enough to have begun it. Besides that, it seemed the Holy Spirit would not allow me to pass on by.

The Midwives Group "Hears into Speech"

The rest of the group shared Whitney and Devena's call to a deeper engagement enabled by divine Hospitality. The two of them had sent a joint e-mail, attaching their correspondence and asking for the group's help. In agreeing, the other Midwives created a process that made obvious and intentional the community's reliance on the presence of Spirit. In her e-mail response Deborah proposed: "We should be sure to take ample time to pray together, both silently and aloud. This may well mean stopping to pray together several times, in addition to starting (and eventually ending) in prayer. . . . We all know from experience that extraordinary things happen in community, especially prayerful community. That knowledge persuades me that we will know what to do."

The conversation itself was an extraordinary example of "hearing into speech," of creating a container that was both supportive and challenging, of experiencing Spirit as Co-inquirer. As Devena and Whitney—embraced by the caring support of the other participants—each articulated their experience of the other, an inner accountability developed. The group became the vehicle in which a creative Hospitality was incarnated. Each of the others brought a Spirit-inspired determination or hope to the process.

Deborah later insisted, "I was not prepared to deal with the loss of either of you from our common intimacy."

Mary K. offered, "I knew if the Spirit was present it would be all right."

Nedi reflected, "The very fact that this was being dealt with openly [gave me] hope."

The outcome was transformative for both women in the conflict. For Whitney the turning point came when she saw Devena "get"—in an "ah-ha" kind of moment—that her confrontational style had made the on-line "conversation" feel unsafe, resulting not in creative engagement but in alienation. Devena's immediate response was astonishment and then sincere regret and sorrow. Whitney felt deeply heard, her feelings honored; the estrangement between them was healed. Devena experienced deep empathy: "Looking intently into her face, I felt [Whit's] pain, I began to cry. Oddly in my crying, Whitney felt heard. Oddly also, in my crying, I felt my strength and the strength of the Midwives. The Midwives held themselves as a vessel of caring for both of us. As one of the new members suggested prayer in silence, I felt a healing comfort stream between us. I name that feeling as 'Holy Spirit.'"

Devena and Whitney both have continued as Midwives, their personal friendship strengthened by their experience of conflict held as it was within the context of Spirit-infused inquiry. The Midwives as a community was transformed as well: our commitment to one another and to our inquiry deepened.

Perhaps this example of en-Spirited action-in-reflection incarnated as no other both the learning and process of our collaborative inquiry. We had, indeed, in this instance, "walked the talk," our meaning-making moving from experience through metaphor into conceptualization and finally effecting real transformation. Between conceptualization and transformation, however, we made crucial choices without which the transformation could not have occurred. These were choices to become and remain—sometimes uncomfortably—vulnerable to one another, choices to trust both our growing capacity as a crucible of creative transformation and our evolving experience of Spirit-within-community. They were the choices of midwives-in-training who found themselves, unexpectedly supported and contained by a spiritual energy, a Hospitality, that acted as Midwife to us all.

References

Heron, J. *Sacred Science: Person-Centered Inquiry into the Spiritual and the Subtle.* Ross-on-Wye: PCCS Books, 1998.

Heron, J. "Transpersonal Co-operative Inquiry." In P. Reason and H. Bradbury (eds.), *Handbook of Action Research.* Thousand Oaks, Calif.: Sage, 2001.

Morton, N. *The Journey Is Home.* Boston: Beacon Press, 1986.

Reason, P. "Sacred Experience and Sacred Inquiry." *Journal of Management Inquiry,* 2 (3), 1993, 273–283.

WHITNEY WHERRETT ROBERSON *is an Episcopal parish priest in Silicon Valley and the founder and coordinator of Spirituality At Work, an action research organization serving business and other professionals.*

6

Jewish women use collaborative inquiry to heal from internalized anti-Semitism. They build community by using action-reflection cycles, wholistic ways of knowing, emotional probing, and validity procedures.

Exploring Internalized Oppression and Healing Strategies

Penny Rosenwasser

Participants: Ten Jewish women, ranging in age from twenty-three to fifty, who identify themselves as progressive activists. We grew up all over the United States and have diverse class and Jewish backgrounds and sexual orientations.

Inquiry purpose: To explore our internalized negative societal messages as Jewish women and to learn how to heal our self-hatred.

Inquiry question: How does internalized Jewish oppression manifest in us, and what are strategies for resisting and healing from this oppression?

Process: Monthly six-hour sessions for ten months. After beginning with traditional action/reflection cycles, we later shifted to embodying healing practices as "actions" during our meetings. To communicate both actions and reflections, we used storytelling, songs, artwork, movement, and theatre. We practiced distress facilitation by incorporating processes for releasing emotions.

Outcomes: We built closeness and community, a powerful antidote to our internalized messages. Realizing that our shared pain resulted from systemic oppression, which was not our fault, emboldened us to become more visible as Jews and to confront anti-Semitism.

> The purpose of human inquiry is not so much the search for truth, but to heal.
>
> —Peter Reason (1994, p.10)

"I have to say, I feel bored with this group," Elly declared at our eighth meeting. She confided that two recent inquiry sessions that had focused on analyzing our learning had felt "heady, not stimulating below the neck. I love seeing all of you," she shrugged, "and this process opened my self-awareness and was exciting for awhile. But when I needed more emotional work, it wasn't there. Sharing our story is the nugget. The work is knowing the questions to ask to get underneath the story."

I convened this inquiry for my doctoral dissertation—and for healing my own internalized anti-Semitism. Internalized oppression is believing the derogatory messages and stereotypes that people outside our group say are true about us. We learn to loathe ourselves, rather than understanding that these destructive beliefs are instilled in us by a socioeconomic political system that constructs us to blame ourselves and our people (Brown, 1995; Hagan, 1993; Schwartz, 1995; Sherover-Marcuse, 1994). I initiated this inquiry because I believe that transforming self-hatred can be liberatory, so that we no longer need accept limits on ourselves, on what we can do, on how the world can be—such inquiry is emancipatory learning (Mezirow, 1991); therefore, healing internalized oppression can also profoundly empower a practice of social action.

I recruited women—by contacting friends, putting ads in publications, and talking about the project—who were passionately interested in exploring how they had internalized beliefs that there was something wrong with them as Jewish women. In my invitation letter, I explained that I was looking for introspective women who were change agents, could commit to one six-hour meeting monthly for ten months, and were seeking community and transformation. In the screening interview, I said I assumed our process would trigger emotions and that we would use healing tools to release these feelings; I asked whether they had skills to facilitate this process. I also asked about their experience with therapy, body-based and personal growth exploration, as well as their experience in groups.

Most of the co-inquirers were seasoned facilitators and all had group experience. At our first meeting, I encouraged the presenting of our knowing through music, art, poetry, and story as part of co-operative inquiry's wholistic epistemology. Everyone shared their healing expertise in voice and movement work, reevaluation counseling, theater, personal coaching, and conflict mediation. We also created guidelines to give us the safety to share vulnerable feelings. During this meeting's reflection Geri revealed she "felt very heard," commenting that she had "never had that experience on this kind of material."

Peter Reason (1988) considers it essential that co-operative inquiry groups establish "a culture in which people can express feelings of anger, grief, fear, and be supported in so doing" (p. 29). Reason (1988) and John Heron (1996) recommend incorporating distress facilitation methods that help members release emotions triggered from past hurts, feelings that can distort meaning-making in the present; this release can then provide fertile ground for creating new knowledge. Like therapy, distress facilitation helps co-inquirers process emotions and, ideally, transform in the process. Unlike therapy, however, co-operative inquiry is a peer process and distress facilitation methods are not the focus of the inquiry; instead, these methods are tools to facilitate learning during action-reflection cycles.

With over twenty-five years of experience in group facilitation and personal growth methods, I introduced reevaluation counseling, or "co-counseling," into our inquiry as a distress facilitation tool. Reason (1994) has referred to co-counseling as a "cathartic discipline" that "provided emotional competence in my own practice" (p. 51). Its premise is that "by using the gifts of healing with which we were born—crying, laughing, shaking, yawning—while someone is listening with kindness and awareness, people are able to heal and flourish" (Freundlich, 2000).

Our group embraced our exploration of internalized oppression with courage and care. We devised actions that experimented with noticing our connection to other Jews; we also viewed movies with Jewish content, examined our racial identities, and told the stories of our Jewish women's bodies.

From this complex experience, I focus on a few significant facets of our inquiry. I audiotaped and transcribed our sessions; using excerpts from transcripts, I illustrate how the co-operative inquiry tools of action-reflection, probing of the emotional realm, presentational construal, and the validity procedures of "devil's advocate" and "sustaining authentic collaboration" served us in our community building and healing.

Exploring the Emotional Realm and Presentational Ways of Knowing During Action-Reflection Cycles

After Elly voiced her frustration with the group, Deena agreed that she wanted our meetings to be "more experiential." "I have new insights," she observed, "but I don't know how to move through them." We decided to refocus on presentational knowing—expressing ourselves through art, music, poetry, theater, dance, and movement—as well as on processing emotions (or distress facilitation), all of which had characterized our earlier sessions.

Acting in Opposition. In the time since our previous meeting, our healing "action" was to "act in opposition" to our internalized anti-Semitism—that is, instead of acting on our old feelings, we had experimented with choosing how we *wanted* to respond to a situation and then *acting* that way!

In sharing her action, Emily told us about teaching at a women's music camp. Fearing that it would bring up old painful feelings of "not belonging," Emily decided this would be a good opportunity to try "acting in opposition."

"When I began to withdraw and get quiet, I asked, 'How would I act if knew I belonged and had a place here?' As a result, I had a different experience in a big group than I've ever had! [I felt] 'I don't have to go away, I can be myself and be here!' By the weekend's end, I felt I had met extended family there, that there's *totally* a place for me."

As we continued sharing our actions, Deena revealed "the safety" she felt in meeting someone who knew about the existence of Iraqi (or Mizrahi–Arab descent) Jews, which was half of her heritage. She realized she needed "to educate people about the complexity of who I am, and then I can feel safe in more places." This experience prompted her, for her action, to paint a watercolor design that would remind her to act in opposition to her internalized feelings of invisibility and not belonging. To create "a call to myself to speak and not stay quiet and resentful," Deena painted "I belong," "You need to know me," and "I'll tell you how to treat me right."

Deena had confided to us previously that she had been speaking quietly and infrequently ever since her seventh grade teacher humiliated her by calling her voice "annoying." When we encouraged Deena to repeat the phrases on her painting *loudly,* as part of "acting in opposition" right there in the group, she laughed (releasing feelings) and spoke louder. "We can't hear you!" we prodded, and Deena spoke more loudly, laughing harder. In this way, we used co-counseling as a distress facilitation practice for exploring the emotional realm, while Deena was both sharing and embodying her action. Since she was releasing feelings, we kept encouraging her. Finally she shouted, "Talking quietly is part of my internalized anti-Semitism 'cause I'm afraid of being loud [of being targeted again]. So you need to know me—and you need to want me!"

As she began to cry, emotions poured out that had been bottled up since seventh grade. "You're doing great!" I encouraged, counseling her to push me as a way to "push those feelings outside of you." She pushed, cried, laughed, and shouted, "You need to know me!"—to which Amy whooped, "I do need to know you!"

We worked with each group member in this way, and during our reflection we noticed how helping one another evoke feelings had expanded our learning about internalized oppression; we also felt closer to each other. "We were doing healing together," Deena pointed out, "supporting one another to feel good about ourselves and take up space and ask for what we need."

Embodying Additional Healing Strategies. To keep responding to Elly's challenge, we decided our next action would be to bring more strategies for healing internalized oppression into the meeting itself. Amy volunteered to create a skit. The next month Amy introduced her skit about "someone who is free of internalized anti-Semitism," asking, "How would she deal with Jews who were still enacting the internalized oppression? It opens up possibilities for how things could be different." As part of our group action of practicing healing strategies during our meeting, we each read a role, and when the script ran out, we improvised. Our dialogue heated up as we brought our own internalized oppression to the characters. When we stopped, as a distress facilitation tool we divided into pairs to process our feelings.

In our group reflection afterwards, Emily appreciated "how the skit pinpointed family dynamics—it got us really involved!" "With all the oppression swirling around," I noticed, "I'm seeing how hard it is not to be triggered by the internalized anti-Semitism, to create a culture of healing." This presentational knowing from participating in the skit gave us new information about our behavior patterns and how we could change them. Noticing what happened when Deena had contradicted her internalized oppression by asking for what she needed in an empowered way instead of acting victimized, I pointed out to her, "Your whole body changed. Your voice got stronger and you seemed centered."

In another example of embodying healing strategies as part of our group action, Emily led us in a tag, follow-the-leader game—again involving us in presentational construal: "I would like us to feel as Jewish women we can take up a lot of space! [to contradict being told that we take up too much space!] Throw out your thinking minds and let yourself play!" Laughter, noise, and running around ensued. Then we began shouting out, and echoing each other:

"Speak loudly!"

"Don't leave me alone."

Our voices softened. "I need you."

"Show me that you like me."

"Let me get close to you."

"Really close."

Now we stood in a circle, with our arms around each other.

"We just want to be together."

"Yeah, closeness."

"I feel how scared I get!"

"But we love you!"

"If I felt people really wanted to be close to me, if I felt I deserved that, I wouldn't be fighting for my life. I could relax."

"What's in the way of being close?"

"We're all terrified."

"I'm afraid of being rejected."

"See how we focus on the negative? We can have thirty positive interactions and one negative one, and we focus on the negative."

"That's our internalized oppression!"

"I'm thinking how deeply I care for all of you," Judith admitted quietly, "and how vulnerable I feel to have you know that. I'm not used to feeling so much permission to be caring."

"Judith, your whole face has opened up!" I exclaimed. "It's neat to see."

"Maybe one of our strategies for healing," Emily suggested, "is saying how much we care for each other."

Many of us expressed later that this was the high point of our inquiry. During our group reflection, I noticed, "It took us nine months to get here—and the more I think about it, at least to do the healing, it's in community. It's building closeness and trust, which just takes time. It's releasing our feelings and incorporating our bodies.

"And the idea of different ways of knowing," I continued, "is that by using different modes, we can get new information."

Emily agreed: "When you start moving and putting your voices together, it connects you physically, it's heart-connected. And it cuts through a lot that can be hard to get through otherwise." It was "tense," she acknowledged, "when we were improvising upon Amy's skit; yet it was also very creative. It opened us in this different way."

"People often feel 'too grown-up' to make silly noises, or 'I don't wanna do a skit,'" Deena added. "But it's in doing them that you learn new things."

Confronting Fear, Embodying Visibility. During another action cycle Amy decided to wear the Jewish skullcap, or yarmulke, in public on the Sabbath, to contradict internalized feelings of marginalization and shame. "I thought, 'What would it be like if somebody knew that I was Jewish from forty feet away?!'" Amy described wearing the yarmulke at her bus stop, "waiting and waiting, and people are getting in a progressively worse humor. The thought flashed into my mind, 'They're gonna blame me [for the late bus], 'cause I'm a scapegoat [as a visible Jew].' I felt like I was making myself into a target; it was the first time I ever came out that way and identified as Jewish, and I was hit with a tidal wave of fear." Amy reported, however, that confronting her fear turned out to be "very positive: Now I feel this pride and confidence in being a Jew that I never had before!"

Continuing to wear the yarmulke every Shabbat, Amy noticed that her willingness to be "that visible" inspired other Jews—and her resulting self-esteem made her adept at confronting the anti-Semitism that came at her. "I'm glad you noticed I'm Jewish," she responded to one antagonist. "Don't you feel it's important to be proud of whatever you are?"

Validity Procedures: Devil's Advocacy and Sustaining Authentic Collaboration

Heron (1996) recommends validity procedures to create findings that are well-grounded and to ensure congruence between ways of knowing and action-reflection. At our second meeting, I introduced these procedures. We consistently spent meeting time noticing whether we had incorporated procedures of challenging uncritical subjectivity, incorporating aspects of reflection, using research cycling, managing unaware projections, accepting chaos, balancing action and reflection time, practicing convergence and divergence in our actions, and sustaining authentic collaboration. Following are examples of our work with "challenging uncritical subjectivity" and "sustaining authentic collaboration."

Challenging Uncritical Subjectivity—or Devil's Advocate. The proverb, "Two Jews, three opinions!" was descriptive of our group and led to engaged meaning-making conversations. We easily incorporated the devil's advocacy procedure of challenging uncritical subjectivity, a process to prevent groups from agreeing before exploring various viewpoints or from making an outcome "fit" because it is expedient.

For example, one or another of us frequently challenged a group assumption that certain behavior was an aspect only of internalized Jewish oppression. From her teaching, Emily asserted that "Women in general are taught not to take up space—vocally, physically—it's not unique to Jews."

Adding to the complexity, Kim pointed out that "Some white non-Jewish women have strong feelings about not being able to break out of the cage [to take up space]. I think Jewish women are more 'out there'—but we're made to feel bad about it."

In a related story, Amy shared, "We were saying [in the group] that there's a Jewish 'thing' about feeling pressure to do things right. The next day I was with a client who's Japanese [non-Jewish], and the same phrases, word for word, were coming out of her mouth. She could have been one of us sitting in the room."

Sustaining Authentic Collaboration—or "Are There Any Influence Hierarchies in the House?" "I'm scared to bring it up, but I noticed we haven't spoken to the validity procedure of paying more attention to one person's thinking than another person's." Halfway through the inquiry I asked our group about the aspect of sustaining authentic collaboration that examines influence hierarchies, that is, whether all group voices are valued equally. I did not anticipate that my question would bring out the ambiguity of my role as group convener-coparticipant who also used our inquiry for my dissertation.

Several members responded saying that they valued different voices at different times. Then Amy unmasked the issue. "I forgot to say the obvious, which is Penny has more influence than the rest. If somebody proposes an idea, and she seconds it, it carries a lot of weight—compared to anybody else seconding it."

I was dumbfounded. "Really?"

"Really!" everyone chorused. "Definitely."

"I didn't realize. Should we do something about that?"

"No, it just is. This is your project."

"But," I protested, "I don't hold the most knowledge about this topic."

"It's not about that."

"Other people hold different parts [of our inquiry] as priority. You hold the whole thing. You don't have more power as much as responsibility."

"The content of what everyone says is heard equally. People concede to you around process, not content."

"You have the bottom-line. You cannot let any part of this slip too far—we know that. It's comforting [laughs]."

Recalling our first meeting, I remembered trying to set up my role so as to prevent having unequal influence. I had acknowledged the complexity inherent in my being the group convener, a group participant, and the "dissertation writer." "But the idea," I had asserted, "is that even when it's obvious that I am invested in a particular process, I have one voice and that's it. Every decision is a group decision."

What had gone wrong? Disoriented, I protested, "I feel like everybody really cares about our inquiry. I trust the group completely."

"That comes across," Kim responded. "You don't hold it in a domineering way. You're saying, 'Here is what I think we need to do.'"

"In terms of our emotional work and our thinking work," Deena added, "it's very much owned [by the group]."

Examining this influence hierarchy continued throughout the inquiry. "You had a foot in each world," Emily observed. "You opened it up for the group to take leadership—and also it was your baby, there were certain things you had to do. But if people wanted to do different things, you were open to that; you wanted everyone to be there fully."

In sharing her appreciation, Emily reveals what I suspect was a prevailing group sensibility; that while this was "our" inquiry, it was also seen as "my" project.

Again Amy spoke frankly, saying it was "odd that there was so much emphasis on how we're all equal, and [yet] you were always going that extra mile for the group in a way that no one else was. I don't think it had a negative impact, but. . . . you could have started us off and then backed off more." She added, "You prompted us through transitions that we needed to go through. I was glad you stepped in, because in a lot of groups people ask, 'What should we do now?' There was also this space where it was very egalitarian. It was a good balance."

What did I learn about being group convener and dissertation writer while trying to create an egalitarian inquiry? That it is important to "turn over" the group *to* the group, encouraging everyone to take responsibility for leadership; to model fluidity and openness; to use my voice consciously, while also examining my attachment to an outcome, and then acknowledging my attachment; to aim for a nonhierarchical process, and then notice how the group chooses to run itself. As one co-inquirer expressed, "I'm appreciating your doing it, and I'm not having to do it." Above all I learned that this process is ambiguous, and the best I can do is attempt to midwife the process without getting in the way.

Implications: What We Learned, How We Changed

"This learning is not about reading by ourselves and going to lectures," M. J. reflected. "Everything we're doing here is an alive process and comes from the heart. That kind of learning makes healing—and when you heal, you feel differently about yourself, so you behave differently in the world. That's happening for me in here."

We found that engaging in action-oriented cycles and reflecting on them, helping each other probe our emotions, employing the wholistic epistemology's multiple ways of knowing, and using validity procedures to examine our process facilitated a profound exploration of our lived experience. These inquiry tools helped us raise our consciousness about Jewish oppression while creating together a vibrant, close community of healing—a contradiction to the isolation, fear, distrust, humiliation, and self-disgust of internalized anti-Semitism. Our new awareness empowered us to take new risks as change agents, and these new actions increased our positive sense of ourselves as Jews—emboldening us to deepen our practice as we transformed our shame into self-esteem.

I personally learned that a fully dimensional learning experience is key to a transformative learning environment—one that engages the physical, cognitive, intuitive, emotional, creative, and spiritual realms—allowing us as learners to access and bring all of ourselves to the inquiry, thus expanding our ability to learn from our experience.

Perhaps Deena's words best illustrate the value of co-operative inquiry as a method for facilitating personal healing in the context of systemic transformation: "Since I've committed my life to social change, the more that I can release and work through—and this group initiated that process—then the more powerful I will be. That feels like a huge shift: the potential to increase my power, rather than just changing my area of work."

References

Brown, C. "Beyond Internalized Anti-Semitism: Healing the Collective Scars of the Past." *Tikkun*, 1995, *10* (2), 44–46.

Freundlich, S. E-mail communication. Oakland, Calif., May 2000.

Hagan, K. L. *Fugitive Information: Essays from a Feminist Hothead*. New York: HarperCollins, 1993.

Heron, J. *Co-operative Inquiry: Research into the Human Condition*. Thousand Oaks, Calif.: Sage, 1996.

Mezirow, J. *Transformative Dimensions of Adult Learning*. San Francisco: Jossey-Bass, 1991.

Reason, P. "The Co-operative Inquiry Group." In P. Reason (ed.), *Human Inquiry in Action: Developments in New Paradigm Research*. Newbury Park, Calif.: Sage, 1988.

Reason, P. "Part I: Towards a Participatory World-View." In P. Reason (ed.), *Participation in Human Inquiry*. Thousand Oaks, Calif.: Sage, 1994.

Schwartz, M. "Truth Beneath the Symptoms: Issues of Jewish Women in Therapy." In K. Weiner and A. Moon (eds.), *Jewish Women Speak Out*. Seattle: Canopy Press, 1995.

Sherover-Marcuse, E. "Liberation Theory: Axioms and Working Assumptions about the Perpetuation of Social Oppression." In N. Gonzalez-Yuen (ed.), *The Politics of Liberation*. Dubuque, Iowa: Kendall-Hunt, 1994.

PENNY ROSENWASSER is a doctoral candidate at the California Institute of Integral Studies in San Francisco and a social justice practitioner.

Women of Color graduate students use CI to explore their educational experience within the academy and relate it to their cultural contexts.

Weaving Our Stories as They Weave Us

Cecilia Pritchard, Pamelaia Sanders

Participants: Students from a graduate school in San Francisco—four of African American heritage and one of Hawai'ian heritage.

Inquiry purpose: To face the challenges of being Women of Color[1] in an institution dominated by Western cultural hegemony.

Inquiry question: What does it mean to be socially engaged, spiritually full Women-of-Color scholars?

Process: Six sessions in eight months.

Outcomes: Implementing on a daily basis the lived reality that education is a form of social activism that is sustained through spiritual practices.

Racism has an impact on every facet of our being: economically, socially, physically, and spiritually. As vocal and sentient beings who are oppressed within this culture, our experience in the particular oppressive context of academia whetted our appetite for this inquiry. Giving voice in a predominately Western culture that more times than not excluded our voices stimulated our desire to gather with other Women of Color. We were attracted to CI as a liberatory methodology that could provide healing, learning, and support through a process of action and reflection.

Two of us, authors of this chapter, co-initiated this inquiry. Our group explored the issues of who we are and how the truths of our cultural, spiritual, and social realities are invited to the table for discussion and representation. We made meaning for ourselves that expanded deeply into our personal lives.

This chapter was written in collaboration with Anasa Jordan, Muhjah Shakir, and Kesha Young.

This chapter is divided into three sections. The first two relate our personal perspectives. Cecilia offers a sweeping account of launching and participating in the inquiry. Pamelaia shares her personal experience of participating in the inquiry and describes how being with the group deepened her learning in a way she would not have experienced had she been by herself. In the last section we engage each other in reflective dialogue.

Cecilia's Story

One of the most critical decisions Pamelaia made was to join with me to create our project. Because I am not African American, she had to shift her original idea from an inquiry with African American women to one with Women of Color. Over several weeks, we spent an enormous amount of time discussing what it means to be a person of color and, more directly, in what ways I met the criteria.

I am biracial. I am mostly of European Hawai'ian heritage and grew up in Hawai'i, where my status as mixed is common and appreciated. As with others of mixed heritage, my physical appearance might be misleading. Although my fair skin has afforded me great privilege and access, it does not change my personal history, experiences, and cultural upbringing. As Pamelaia and I shared our families' stories, to my surprise I found myself disclosing difficulties in my family around racism, challenges of being first generation in college, my own sense of alienation in graduate school, and my deep-seated experiences of internalized oppression. The depth of our sharing surprised both of us and allowed us to become clearer about how we felt regarding the emerging topic.

At this point we had two different topics in mind but decided to move forward by inviting individuals to explore both topics jointly. We settled on three other graduate students and approached them to join us in examining the topics of "exploring the experience of Women of Color as scholars" and "an inquiry into social activism as a spiritual path." We were fortunate; just uttering the two topics to the invited women excited them. I believe the significant elements of the two inquiries guided our invitation process. Intuitively we approached Women of Color who were not only scholars (graduate students) but women who had rich spiritual lives and strong commitments to social justice. By the time we got together as a group, Pamelaia and I had a clearer idea of what our joint topic was; we had begun to refer to the inquiry as "exploring what it means to be socially active, spiritually full, Women-of-Color scholars."

We were ready to go. There would be five of us. Pamelaia and I were excited to get started. Committed to holding our roles as facilitators lightly, we hoped that our group would develop shared leadership and ownership for what we were creating.

Coming together as a group was easy and delicious. For our first session we gathered at my house and sat in my mother's formal dining room, using our best china for a dinner we had brought to the table. It was a special occasion and we could feel it in the air around us. We built an altar in the center of the table and included items from our ancestors, nature, and various spiritual traditions. We knew this experience was a rare and extraordinary gift we were giving ourselves.

Our participation as a group has yielded three cycles of action and reflection thus far. Questions seem to come to us naturally through the sharing of our stories and ease of our conversations. Our first inquiry question was, *Who am I?* The action we took was to observe how our daily lives informed the question. When we came back together, one of us had had a powerful dream, which led to a discussion about the meaning of the dream's content as well as the meaning of dreams in our lives. It was no surprise that our second action would be to record our dreams as response to the new question, *What do I believe in?* Our experiences with the dreams at first appeared to be interesting stories with little in common. The more we talked about them, the more we found shared themes: profoundly knowing our life's purposes while deeply questioning our capacity to fulfill these purposes.

This knowledge has led us to a new action of pulling daily a spread of three Black Angel cards, an oracle developed and published by Earthlyn Manuel (1999). We respond to three questions: *How does my suffering emerge? What process of transformation moves me from the sleeping path to the waking path? Where do I find joy?* We are in the midst of this last action and it is yielding rich results.

As we develop our own rhythm around cycles of action, reflection, and meaning-making, we notice much of our sharing is through storytelling. We come to life when we tell stories, often raising our voices and rousing our bodies. We speak deliberately, sometimes no louder than a whisper and other times as loud as thunder. We tell stories whenever we have something important to share, and these stories always seem to intimate something bigger than ourselves emerging in the circle.

We invoke the telling of stories out of what seems to be a natural way of participating together. Engaging with our stories allows us to learn more deeply about each other, our communities, and ourselves in the larger world. We make meaning from reflection on these stories. One of our key findings from making sense of our experience has been, *Education for us is a form of social activism and we sustain ourselves through our spirituality.*

Coming to this meaning has been a journey of sharing our stories about our parents and the generations before us. We shared their experiences of living in a world that often did not appreciate who they were and what they offered. There were stories of courage, struggle, and mastery. Many of these stories had been handed down for generations, linking us to the beliefs and values of our families and cultures. As we told our stories, we were becoming a container for them so that we might be able to pass them on to our children. Telling each other our stories wove a rich quilt and a larger narrative of those who have gone before us. We were all in graduate school as part of a purpose larger than our own individual education. We were here as part of a long journey of emancipation through education, which started long before our births—before the first generation of our ancestors stepped through the doors of a schoolhouse. Remembering their struggles and honoring our foreparents somehow fuels the drive to complete our education.

Pamelaia's Story

I recall the emotional highs and lows of my first semester in graduate school. It had been twelve years since I completed my undergraduate degree—deep in the heart of Louisiana. I spent many years studying various areas of interest that enhanced my knowledge base. Life had taught me numerous lessons as well. I now intended to use those lessons in a way that would render my living a wholistic life. Graduate school was to be my time for experiencing my love of learning from a different perspective.

I had been immersed in a mainstream hierarchical educational system and societal structure for the major portion of my life (Craige, 1992). At this point in the venture, I was ready to state where I stood on issues: to challenge, question, and offer an alternative voice to the hierarchical discourse that has dictated mainstream thinking. I did not want to repeat in graduate school what happened in undergraduate school. History wanted to repeat itself within my experiences.

My interest as an African American woman enmeshed in my Southern culture and spiritual belief system centers around empowering self and establishing voice for myself and other women of the African Diaspora as we matriculate in the academy. My life work focuses on marginalized and oppressed communities of peoples of color. In using CI, I hoped to create a space of wholistic learning, healing, and growth intellectually, personally, and professionally. Our research group provided structure for that and much more.

There is something to be said when women scholars gather to build community with one another. There were and still are soul healing benefits from our being together to create meaning for ourselves. The multidimensionality of the women and the broad base of our experiences rendered a space in which we could learn from, support, and share our own knowledge base.

We made meaning for ourselves in telling our individual and collective stories. Many of the stories were continuing monologues, dialogues, and dreams from experiences in our personal and professional lives. Early in our CI relationship Cecilia and I had begun to share our dreams with one another from a cultural perspective. In the group we did action and reflection exercises in recording our dream life. I recall the night I shared the dream that has resurfaced in my life for several years.

I've recorded my dream life for some time now and felt the need to share one dream that remains constant and unchanged. As I told the dream and remembered its details, I traveled to an emotional space in remembering the feeling of isolation and my need to understand the symbolic meaning that my psyche was transmitting to my subconscious. Tears formed in my eyes. My co-researchers gathered around me; they witnessed and embraced my telling of this dream. Within the CI, I formed meaning for myself and understood profoundly that I was to use all of my resources (spiritual, communal, intellectual) to sustain me on this liberatory path of empowerment.

> I stood crouched over—peeping through the keyhole of a large wooden door that blocked my entrance into the main room. Fear embraced my entire being and isolated me from the knowledge that could be obtained on the other side. I felt isolated and frightened, realizing that there was no one to welcome me or to walk with me through the door.
>
> I stood alone in this dark, dank, musty entrance, sensing that I was being beckoned to enter and dwell within this enlightening place of wisdom. Light emanated from each corner of the waiting room. My arrival had been expected. I had journeyed a long distance to get to this particular location. I was to be there. The path had been paved for me.
>
> This ancient dwelling was an expansive palace. My spirit traveled through the dusty chambers where great works of art, history, science, philosophy, and religion had been studied, written, and created. Only a few had entered into the deeper compartments of this mystical place. A welcoming banquet had been prepared. Why was I on the outside of the threshold gazing through—only to see a fragment of this enormous place?
>
> I kept coming to this same location; time and time again, year after year. Each time, I questioned, How will I transcend this barrier that stands between me and the space that has been prepared for me? Who has constructed this obstacle that keeps my voice from being heard and my physical presence from entering the room? If I were to enter, I would have to muster up the strength to stand: physically and intellectually to announce my arrival and prepare for the journey that was ahead.

The time has come for me to enter and make my presence known within academia. The dream has become reality. I am sitting within the halls of academia pursuing my goal of being an educator, a voice for change and empowerment within the global community. The relevant information for entering this domain is knowing that I am not alone on the journey, nor have I ever been alone. Others have traveled the road before me and have made enormous sacrifices—just so I can be here today. I cannot survive the journey in isolation. There are others within the educational community who join me in the work that we are doing in the world. Together we listen and learn from and with one another to support the efforts in our shared journeys.

Weaving Our Stories

CECILIA: In participating in our CI, I learned and was reminded about what education has meant to each of our people. Particularly the struggle. And how education has been political action for us. That it was not a given—and is still very much not a given when it comes to higher education. The more time I spend with you and our group, the more I get, "Oh yeah, this is political action." Just being here, walking in these corridors, just saying "I'm going to be here in my fullness."

PAMELAIA: Walking in your own power. In your own history. In your own way of being.

CECILIA: That I'm coming to this as a cultural equal. As someone who comes from another culture that creates knowledge and meaning for its community. That these are also the stories of our foreparents and even though our own stories and our histories may be different it is essentially the same story.

PAMELAIA: When you say that, I am reminded of my parents. I'm blessed in having both of my parents with me. Daddy often talks about when he was a young boy growing up. There were people who looked like him who were his teachers. He knew these women and they knew his parents. The way they walked in the world was important. They supported the community, the people, and the village. I think it is important to see people around me who look like me. And I think about my mother sharing stories of walking many miles to school, seeing the white children on buses while they walked in the cold.

As we go through this CI, I realize this generation, which includes my older siblings and myself, has been blessed to be able to obtain our education. It's a privilege to have completed my master's and now be working on my Ph.D. I understand that there are still barriers to overcome. My older sisters integrated the high school I graduated from. And I realize the things I have had to deal with in graduate school. Here I am a black woman working on her Ph.D. in a white male academy. I say to myself, "Hey, you've an awesome responsibility, girlfriend. As others have paved the way, you too must pave the way for others. You're blessed to be here!"

I remember the night I shared my dream with you all. In so many ways, I feel as an educator, and as I become an academician, I am an outsider wanting to be on the inside. We are Women and People of Color who are becoming scholars. To be affirmed by the CI group, to have you all hear me and embrace my being, that was liberating on many levels because I began to understand differently my purpose for being here. I remember crying and then telling myself, "It's OK, you don't have to stand outside looking through the peephole. You have the right to walk through the doors of academia and to have voice and be affirmed." I remember having that dream for a long time.

CECILIA: What was really powerful was that yours and Anasa's and Kesha's dreams had a similar theme. It seems to me that CI allows people to come together and find some of their experiences are not isolated. That's what is powerful. Sometimes you get a glimpse of your own power but when you hear it in the collective it seems to take on an unspeakable size, bigger than just the collection of us.

PAMELAIA: And to realize we are not on this path alone.

CECILIA: It's like we're all one step up and one step down. If I look in front of me there is always someone giving me a hand and if I look behind me, there's always someone needing my hand.

PAMELAIA: And no hand is in isolation.

CECILIA: Exactly. I have also been thinking about cycles of action, reflection, and meaning-making. I think that happens naturally in our cultures. We go out and whether we have declared it or not, we take a common action. Be it going to graduate school, getting a job, or being the first in that job. Whatever it is, it is an action. And then we come together and reflect upon that together, and make meaning that sustains us to go back out in the world.

PAMELAIA: And this is about working together as a community. This process can be taken out into other communities. We are five in number and we five women can go out and create other CI groups.

CECILIA: This is where I have a question. How is this different from other forms of community? Or is it? Did we really do something different in calling it CI? Maybe we are just five Women-of-Color graduate students who got together to share our experiences.

PAMELAIA: We knew we were going to do a CI. But the thing is we had a different approach. We were involved with this process even as we were going about our daily lives. At least I was. And I think the other women would say the same, as well.

CECILIA: We all came in with the agreement that we would do a CI. In its simplest form, we would have an inquiry, take an action, reflect upon it together and make shared meaning. It became such a natural process that it makes me question if we did anything.

I suspect that for our communities we know no other way of being. I really do believe it is a part of our cultural context. We often go out and take action and reflect upon things together. It has been nice of John Heron to make it into a methodology but I think it's a deep part of our heritage.

PAMELAIA: I agree with you. I remember listening to the stories of my mother and older sisters when they were involved with the civil rights movement. The community came together, talked about what needed to be done, and then went back out in the world and did things.

CECILIA: Why yes, the entire civil rights movement was born taking action, reflecting on it, making meaning, and going back out there.

PAMELAIA: Exactly. That's been a part of my life, my mother's, my siblings'.

CECILIA: Your birthright. The civil rights movement was founded on action and reflection. Its primary movers and shakers like Malcolm X and Martin Luther King were also very spiritually grounded. It was a spiritual movement. As Ghandi's was.

PAMELAIA: In our inquiry group, even though we have different spiritual practices we see each other as spiritual beings and our connected collective consciousness in the world.

CECILIA: Do you remember my original topic? It was to honor the philosophies and practices of Martin Luther King, Jr. and Mohandas Ghandi during the Season of Non-Violence? To me they are the embodiment of CI. Their lives were dedicated to taking action, reflecting, and making meaning in their communities.

PAMELAIA: We were making meaning collectively in the sharing of our stories.

CECILIA: I think that somehow it boils down to the stories and the narratives. I believe Heron's got something with his theory of extended epistemology. If we could just get the stories out. When I'm telling a story I'm not often sure what is going to come out. It's not a script and I'm not worried about facts. When I'm telling a story, I'm conveying the deepest parts of the experience.

I also believe it's a testament to the ability of our cultures to produce and use knowledge in our communities. We tell our story as a way of teaching our people about what is useful in our cultural practices and as a way of creating knowledge that will allow our communities to flourish. It is always about the flourishing of the whole community, not the flourishing of one individual. We assume the way an individual flourishes is when you make sure that the community flourishes. That's why CI works in our cultural settings because CI privileges collective reflection and meaning-making.

PAMELAIA: I take with me, from this richly woven experience of being in our CI, an even greater appreciation of not only my people's histories as African Americans, but an expanded consciousness of the cultures that make this world a global village. I believe what I hear myself embracing is the multiple ways of viewing the world and the multiple truths that connect us. It's about generative, sustainable, and viable communities. That's the hallmark of CI.

Note

1. Women of Color is capitalized to indicate a proper name and a socially constructed concept that delineates a distinctive and identifiable group of individuals.

References

Craige, B. J. *Laying the Ladder Down: The Emergence of Cultural Holism.* Amherst: University of Massachusetts Press, 1992.
Manuel, E. M. *Black Angel Cards: A Soul Revival Guide for Black Women.* San Francisco: Harper, 1999.

CECILIA PRITCHARD *is an educator, coach, and consultant working with both individuals and groups. She has over thirty years of experience in both corporate and nonprofit settings. Currently, Cecilia is a doctoral student at the California Institute of Integral Studies in San Francisco.*

PAMELAIA SANDERS *has worked for over fifteen years as a social change agent within the global community. Her creative passions include writing, singing, teaching, and gardening. She is currently pursuing a doctorate at the California Institute of Integral Studies in San Francisco.*

8

Separate groups pursue inquiries into the impact of White hegemony on participants' lives. This project's unique infrastructure supports learning that leads to changed beliefs and new behaviors.

A Multiple-Group Inquiry into Whiteness

European-American Collaborative Challenging Whiteness

> *Participants:* Thirteen groups and fifty participants, including faculty, adult students, and community members. Some participants earn academic credit.
>
> *Inquiry purpose:* For participants, to develop personal understanding about what it means to be a member of the dominant group in society and to translate new understanding into changed behavior and social action. For the institution, to improve environment for diversity.
>
> *Process:* Most groups meet face to face but several participate on-line via private electronic conference. Inquiries typically run for nine months; new groups form each year. Each group determines its own action-reflection cycles. Infrastructure that supports multiple groups includes community gatherings, shared reflection papers, on-line communication among all participants, and a representative planning committee.
>
> *Outcomes:* Participants report changed beliefs and behaviors, including more effective communication with other White people about racism. Many describe a new sense of community that alleviates the isolation, despair, and guilt they have often associated with challenging their own racism.

When an issue arises about which members of a community recognize they need to foster learning, the federated application of collaborative inquiry may be a useful strategy. The need for better ways to address issues of racism and White privilege in a small graduate school inspired the creation of this multiple-group structure, which we believe is unique.

NEW DIRECTIONS FOR ADULT AND CONTINUING EDUCATION, no. 94, Summer 2002   © Wiley Periodicals, Inc.

Birth of the Project

The birth of the project occurred during a student-led workshop that focused on raising awareness about how White[1] supremacist norms and consciousness dominate U.S. culture. During the workshop, a group of faculty and students of Color[1] decided to create a course in which people of Color could affirm their distinct cultural ways of knowing and being as scholars. Their decision inspired a group of White people to initiate a parallel course to help White people understand the impact of White supremacist consciousness on their lives. Through a series of meetings, the White group chose co-operative inquiry (CI) as a method for structuring the project because CI engages learners in focusing on their own lived experience.

Controversial Decisions

Two elements in this project have been especially controversial: (1) our use of the term *White supremacist* and (2) the separation of the project into two sections, one for Whites and one for people of Color.

Why "White Supremacist"? We are often approached by White people who sincerely want to join a dialogue about racism but who are alienated by the word *supremacist*. We believe it is important to use this emotionally charged phrase. In common usage, *White supremacist* refers to extremists who advocate racial separatism based on their conscious conviction that White people are superior human beings; these White supremacists typically advocate hatred of non-White peoples. We use the term *White supremacist consciousness* not to refer to a group of people but to a system of thought. White supremacist consciousness describes a way of thinking that takes for granted the legitimacy of an American society dominated by White norms and values. In other words, White norms and values are normalized, thus making implicit their supremacy over other groups' norms and values. It is this normalization that maintains the institutionalization of privilege based on race.

Our impetus to use this highly charged phrase comes from people of Color, drawn from the discourse of *Critical Race Theory* (Delgado, 1995). As critical race discourse observes, many in our society fail to understand that racism is the institutionalization of privilege, not simply a manifestation of prejudiced attitudes by individuals. When well-intentioned White people see themselves as "not prejudiced" they often assume they are also "not racist" because they are examining their personal attitudes instead of the way in which they participate in unjust distributions of power and privilege based on race.

We acknowledge that the extremists and the well intentioned are motivated by different concerns—the former advocating hate and superiority, the latter respect and equality. What is important for understanding supremacist consciousness is not people's intentions but the practical impact of the underlying system of thought described above. This system of thought permeates representations of race in the media and institutional structures in the United States by shaping the beliefs and actions of extremists and the well-intentioned alike. Despite their apparent and genuine differences, the two groups share similar assumptions about the superiority of White norms and values, differing only because these assumptions are explicit and overt with one group, implicit and unconscious with the other. That this supremacist consciousness is often invisible to the well-intentioned only strengthens it as a force for oppression. Identifying structural racism not only inside society but also in the most well-intentioned of individuals has been humbling for participants in the project and represents an important aspect of the learning that has taken place.

Why Two Sections? The separation of the project into race-based groups—especially the "White only" section, with its echoes of segregation and the separate-but-equal policies that dominated the United States for the century after the Civil War—is also controversial. This separation continues to be challenged by some White participants and by the wider institutional community. Questions are consistently raised about whether members of a dominant group can learn about themselves in isolation, or whether oppressive behaviors will remain invisible or, worse, be reinforced. The decision to separate arose from both principle and circumstance. It has turned out to be a positive aspect of the experience and intrinsic to the learning that has taken place.

The initial organizers of the project assumed that those who benefit from White skin privilege have a responsibility to confront racism in themselves and society. Both people of Color and Whites felt that if White people, rather than relying on people of Color, accepted more responsibility for and could direct their own learning about racism, greater equity would be realized. When the people of Color elected to meet separately, indicating their need for a safe haven as a necessary antidote to feelings of isolation that they experience in largely White academic settings, their decision created a challenging circumstance: Whites would need to find a way to engage the questions with one another, if they were to engage at all.

The decision to use CI, with its emphasis on common experience and its explicitly nonhierarchical structure, was deemed to hold potential for confronting rather than avoiding the concerns raised about Whites meeting together. All groups report that the CI process creates a context of trust such that participants are able to become vulnerable enough to acknowledge and examine felt experiences of racist thoughts and behaviors, learn from them, and change. This process is clearly facilitated by, if not reliant on, the Whites-only nature of the groups. This is not to suggest that we imagine that the fundamental challenge of confronting racism lies in this transformation process alone. Organizers have seen it as a complement to, not a replacement for, other multicultural learning experiences. Many participants simultaneously pursue other forms of diversity studies.

People of Color express appreciation that White people are meeting in separate groups, seeing it as an indication that Whites are becoming more conscious of how they must change in relation to race. From working with other White people, White participants report that they feel better able to act as allies in multicultural settings.

Learning Outcomes

During the project's second year, one group initiated case study research to discover how the project had affected the first year's participants. Learning outcomes for individual participants, which are described more fully elsewhere (Barlas and others, 2000a, 2000b), include the following: increased capacity to be trusting, vulnerable, and self-reflective; new use of language for conversing about race; increased knowledge about White norms; changes in behavior in work and personal settings; increased sense of community with White people; and increased compassion for self and others.

Participants describe growth and change irrespective of their different initial states of awareness. Some acknowledge that when they began participating in CI, they were completely unconsciousness regarding White normative behavior and White privilege; others began with an acute conscious awareness coupled with disdain for White people who remain ignorant about racism. No matter what quality of initial awareness characterized the participant, all but one reported a change in awareness associated with the CI experience.

The inquiry process helps participants develop capacity for critical self-reflection. Conducting CI actions, as for example "noticing what happens to you when someone makes a racist comment in your presence," brings the inquiry into people's daily lives. Eleanor described this experience as an "expanded instant" when her mind slows because she has heard someone say something racist. She referred to it as a "psychological internal space" and said, "It feels almost like an infinitely large little moment and then it collapses and then you have to go on with chronological time."

Using a photography metaphor, Gretchen explained, "It's like I'm doing something and all of a sudden I get a snapshot of myself doing it. . . . I'm still moving but I see myself frozen in this one place in time and it kind of haunts me."

The CI actions helped Eleanor and Gretchen pay attention to particular moments; the reflection that followed in their CI groups helped them make shared meaning of their experience.

Participants are able to use their CI groups as a place to practice new language and behaviors; they notice that the vulnerability they allow themselves within their CI groups enables them to admit their ignorance and fears, leading them toward the courage to use new language and take action in other contexts of their lives. Andrew reported, "There is no question that my work in this group affects the language I use and the way I speak about the experience of internalized self-hatred and seeing myself as the oppressor. . . . I now have ways to talk about White supremacy with people that I didn't have before, new language, new metaphors and images."

Sarah, who was in her fourth year of a doctoral program in multicultural education, spoke about how she learned to risk "not looking good." She believes that her participation contributed importantly to her ability to speak authentically. She noted that the humility and compassion of others in her inquiry group, especially of those she had perceived as "having it mastered," allowed her to talk about her experience and learn from her mistakes.

Increased confidence in carrying the discourse of White supremacist consciousness into social interactions is exemplified by Victoria, who explained that because of her CI group she is learning to be more effective in speaking with other White people about Whiteness. Now she sees herself more often seeking to stay "in relationship" as she converses with White people about White supremacist norms, rather than what she saw herself doing previously—preaching and assuming a right-wrong dichotomous stance. She recalled talking with a family member about race. "I was trying to listen really hard to what his point of view was so that I wouldn't slam any doors. . . . I had a different notion inside my head about what I was trying to do than I had before I came into this group."

Victoria's CI group labeled the attitude of preaching and scorning as wanting to be "the good White person" who can feel superior to "the bad White person." Daniel, who was in Victoria's CI group, explained that the idea of "the good White person" continues to influence his everyday life two years later.

Eleanor described how her experience in her CI group motivated her to become a catalyst for change in the community college where she teaches. Inspired by Eleanor's activism, other faculty and staff became reengaged in a diversity committee and received a grant to create a diversity program.

In some cases it is difficult for people to attribute changes solely to this inquiry project, since many are also working at "unlearning racism" in other ways. However, nearly all participants affirmed the impact of CI. Gretchen explained, "The change in consciousness from this inquiry is subtle and slight at times to booming insights at other times."

Process for Organizing a Multiple-Group Inquiry

A federated design supports the learning outcomes described above. The project has been shepherded by Linda Sartor, who is both the project coordinator and the instructor for participants enrolled for academic credit. Linda's approach to guiding this complex project is influenced by her own research into how collaborating groups can be facilitated in ways that equalize internal power dynamics (Sartor, 1998).

We use the term *shepherding* to capture the spirit of Linda's leadership. This multiple-group project fosters self-direction and collaboration not only within the individual groups but also in the larger supportive infrastructure. Participants share responsibility for group leadership and decision making; the project coordinator is available for direction and support.

Getting Started. The project begins each year with an open kick-off meeting. Since the project coordinator is not present in the inquiry groups once they begin, she has a limited opportunity to influence and support the groups. Linda feels that this meeting is "a critical element in the functioning of the whole project." Therefore, we describe this element of the multiple-group structure in detail.

People are invited into the project through written documents or word of mouth, which usually includes the phrase "White supremacist consciousness." Consequently, when Linda begins working with the groups she presumes that participants who join "already accept that White supremacist norms and consciousness exist in our lives as members of the dominant culture, and that participants have the desire to 'do' something about this awareness."

People come to the kick-off meeting to learn more about the project. Linda describes four intentions for the day: (1) to deepen relationships among potential members in the context of White supremacist consciousness, (2) to create a shared understanding of co-operative inquiry, (3) to establish each person's commitment to the project, and (4) to help participants make critical decisions that will support group functioning.

Attendees share deeper stories of their own White supremacist consciousness. Then they discuss why strong commitment is essential: the emotional intensity generated from inquiring into one's own White supremacist consciousness is challenging; participants can slip into denial and be motivated to find reasons to "have to miss" a CI meeting. Linda provides handouts about CI and spends time explaining its validity procedures, extended epistemology, and John Heron's application of the Apollonian and Dionysian cultures of group functioning (1996, pp. 45–49).

Inquiry groups form after lunch and conduct their first meeting during the rest of the day. Linda encourages each group to develop capacity for and ownership of the CI process among its members. The newly formed groups spend the rest of the day addressing the following items: (1) articulating an inquiry question, (2) identifying the group's first action, (3) selecting meeting times and places, (4) clarifying a confidentiality agreement, (5) planning for distress facilitation (Reason, 1988; Heron, 1996), and (6) identifying a representative to the planning committee.

Consistent with the design of CI, from then on the groups are self-facilitating and Linda is not involved in their internal procedures. In order to continue to support the groups, she relies on several elements of infrastructure, outlined below.

Providing Support. Five structural elements in this multiple-group project keep the coordinator informed about what is happening within each group and also help the groups create a larger sense of community. These elements are the planning committee, the end-of-year symposium, reflection papers, an on-line community space, and group progress reports.

The planning committee meets on a regular basis. At least one participant of each group serves as a representative to this committee; all participants are welcome. Planning committee meetings provide cross-fertilization among groups as well as an opportunity for Linda to stay in touch with what is happening within each group. The planning committee meetings also generate enthusiasm, commitment, and a sense of ownership for the project. In the spirit of CI, the leadership of the planning committee is intentionally collaborative. Planning committee members make decisions for the project as a whole, grappling with such issues as publicity, sustainability, and recruitment.

The committee also plans an end-of-year symposium that brings all the White group participants together for a day. The first end-of-year event gave each group an opportunity to present its work in progress. Groups used presentational modalities of storytelling, dramatizations, and visual art to describe members' growing insights about White supremacist norms and the way in which the CI process supported their learning. The whole gathering then reflected on the presentations, thus casting the symposium as a multiple-system cycle for action, reflection, and new meaning-making. For the second end-of-year symposium, project participants invited friends and colleagues to participate in a variety of activities that employed the extended epistemology (Heron, 1996) to explore White supremacist consciousness.

Brooke expresses appreciation for the symposium because of the sense of community that it brought her: "I loved the way we all came together at the end to have the symposium. . . . There was a sense that the community we were building in our small groups could be reflected by a larger group of committed participants that shared our learning experience."

Eleanor explains, "Sharing with the bigger [symposium] group is like practice. I carry that with me." Overall, having multiple inquiry groups seems to lend momentum to the project.

For those taking the inquiry project for credit, writing and sharing reflection papers affects the learning of individuals as well as the learning of their groups. Reflection papers also allow Linda to track and contribute to the CI experiences. Daniel, who was the only member of his group earning academic credit, explains: "[The reflection paper] gave me another chance to reflect and make meaning on the process and thus contributed to my own learning as well as what I brought to the group. . . . Feedback comments from Linda on my required writings provided supportive input from a source outside of the group. For example, I remember the critical discussion about power dynamics that was set off in the group due to one of Linda's comments on one of my reflection papers." Such input from an outsider can stimulate validity processes that help a group constructively challenge the meaning it is making of its experience.

Regular on-line communication in a private conference provides participants with an opportunity to discuss the topic with members of other CI groups. In addition, Linda sends periodic e-mail updates to the entire community of past and current participants.

A group progress report is required at the end of each semester. All members within a group who are participating for academic credit collaborate in creating the report. This report helps Linda stay informed about each group's experience.

Conclusions

White people often mask their experience from themselves. When that experience is related to race, racism, privilege, or hegemony, the motive to separate themselves from their experience is strong. This multiple-group project in which White people focus on understanding their own participation in White supremacist norms and consciousness has been a catalyst for individual and group learning. Participants identify changes both in their personal capacities and in their professional practices.

We identify several characteristics of this project's multiple-group design that can be useful to practitioners considering adapting this strategy for their own organizational or community learning needs.

• Focusing on an organizational or community issue that requires expanded awareness rather than problem solving
• Providing meticulous attention to the formation of each group
• Reinforcing the commitment of members to the group
• Utilizing collaboration on all levels and phases of the project
• Implementing multiple structures for intergroup communications through which CI processes can be monitored
• Using cycles of action and reflection learning throughout infrastructure, as in the symposium and planning committee

The project coordinator plays an important role in monitoring and supporting the CI process. For example, Linda helps groups manage their use of validity procedures and experience-based learning processes. As our dominant learning culture tends to privilege conceptual analysis and discourse, new inquirers may require extra support to stay grounded in learning from their own experience by using presentational as well as propositional forms of knowing. The shepherding role is made easier if there are some participants who have prior CI experience.

In this project, Linda's dual role of project coordinator and instructor creates a challenge. Evaluation of student performance conflicts with the self-directed and participatory nature of the CI process. Although the dual role is not ideal, it creates benefits. Information generated from the course requirements of progress reports and reflection papers helps her know what kinds of support are needed for the groups.

One principle of the CI process is that outcomes emerge from the practice and are not *a priori*. Thus, facilitators must recognize they have no control over outcomes. A multiple-group CI can promote organizational change but it is different from other forms of action research because there is no specific problem to be solved. With CI, changes in individual consciousness may affect the larger organization or system, but the nature of those changes can be neither predicted nor controlled. The degree to which these CI groups actually learn as a collective, rather than learning solely at the individual level, provides an interesting question for further attention. Because this project is only in its third year, we cannot yet gauge what impact it may have on fostering cultural change within the institution as a whole system.

Note

1. The words *Color* and *White* are socially constructed designations and constitute proper names; thus they merit capitalization. When these words are written in lower case they and their social significance are "normalized" as ordinary adjectives, obscuring their social meaning and significance. Our capitalization is intended to help the reader stay aware of these designations as social constructions.

References

Barlas, C., Kasl, E., Kyle, R., MacLeod, A., Paxton, D., Rosenwasser, P., and Sartor, L. "Learning to Unlearn White Supremacist Consciousness." *Proceedings of the 41st Annual Adult Education Research Conference*. Vancouver, British Columbia, Canada: The University of British Columbia, 2000a.

Barlas, C., Kasl, E., Kyle, R., MacLeod, A., Paxton, D., Rosenwasser, P., and Sartor, L. "Co-operative Inquiry as a Facilitator for Perspective Transformation." *3rd International Transformative Learning Conference Proceedings*. New York: Teachers College, Columbia University, 2000b.

Delgado, R. (ed.). *Critical Race Theory: The Cutting Edge*. Philadelphia: Temple University Press, 1995.

Heron, J. *Co-operative Inquiry: Research into the Human Condition*. Thousand Oaks, Calif.: Sage, 1996.

Reason, P. "The Co-operative Inquiry Group." In P. Reason (ed.), *Human Inquiry in Action: Developments in New Paradigm Research*. Newbury Park, Calif.: Sage, 1988.

Sartor, L. "Collaboration and How to Facilitate It: A Co-operative Inquiry." *Dissertation Abstracts International*, 58 (11), 441. University Microfilms No. 9814533, 1998.

EUROPEAN-AMERICAN COLLABORATIVE CHALLENGING WHITENESS fosters research and learning about the subject of White supremacist consciousness. Members, who came together originally as participants in a cultural consciousness project at the California Institute of Integral Studies in San Francisco, are Carole Barlas, Elizabeth Kasl, Alec MacLeod, Doug Paxton, Penny Rosenwasser, and Linda Sartor. Past member Roberta Kyle is an important contributor to our knowledge construction. Inquiries about the Collaborative's work can be addressed via e-mail to collaborative@eccw.org.

Multiple collaborative inquiry groups are established within a school to provide structure for facilitating professional development and improving practice.

9

Uniting Teacher Learning: Collaborative Inquiry for Professional Development

John N. Bray

Participants: Six groups and twenty-three participants, all teachers in a small rural K-12 public school. After one group's success in the initial year, five new groups formed during the following academic year.

Inquiry purpose: Each group formed around a distinctive inquiry question. Individual group questions included inquiry about how teachers could improve their practice, incorporate technology into the classroom, change the local school culture, use collaborative inquiry (CI), and alter the structure of the middle school for improved student learning.

Process: Groups had no formalized interaction. Each met for a single academic year, consisting of nine cycles of action and reflection.

Outcomes: Inquiry group outcomes were multifaceted. They included: (1) invigoration of individual teachers for renewed efforts at self-improvement, (2) creation of a network of teacher interaction where isolation previously existed, (3) change in teachers' classroom behavior, and (4) both structural and cultural change in the school itself.

My experience as a CI initiator persuades me to conclude that participative inquiry is the best hope for teachers taking responsibility for their learning environment and, consequently, for producing meaningful, enduring results in teacher development. My belief is supported by the Glenn Commission (2000), which advocates in its report *Before It's Too Late* that teacher inquiry groups should be held as sacrosanct in teacher development!

Collaborative Inquiry in Teacher Development

Teachers in our school believe that collaborative inquiry furnishes a powerful learning strategy because it offers a context-sensitive methodology for learning our way out of workplace difficulties. Our teachers often state that their day-to-day work experience needs nourishment and direction, perhaps even re-ignition. We take pride in our accomplishments as teacher-researchers engaged in CI. My experience has been that as collaborative inquirers our teachers eagerly participate from beginning to end and then look forward for more. This chapter describes how CI was established in our school and the impact it has had on the teachers as adult learners.

Negotiating the Arrangements

As initiator of the CI project, my primary need at the onset of the inquiry was to have a vision about CI's potential for addressing our school's deficiencies as an educational community. Matching the needs of our school with my understanding of CI provided me with the stimulus to proceed.

In commencing the inquiry process, my first question was, *Is there interest among our teachers?* For me, person-to-person contact seemed the best way to ascertain the answer. With the addition of three or more colleagues, we would be ready to start. Eight teachers responded to my invitation.

Most teachers do not have it within their power to arrange for off-site meetings and school release time. Our teachers unanimously agreed that both were essential for inquiry success. Not only did they believe it important to be undistracted by possible intrusion from the work environment, but more important, they noted that teachers generally participate in in-service development activities during the regular work day, typically in professional conference settings. They believed the legitimacy of their inquiry as professional development would be symbolized by the administration's support for release time and off-site meeting space. Therefore, I consulted with the administration about our needs.

During the time our six groups met we had three administrators, each of whom had different concerns. Accordingly, each administrator had to be approached somewhat differently. Common concerns of the administrators included

- How much time is needed?
- What will the inquiry cost?
- What are the demonstrable benefits for the district?
- What is the public perception of district and administrator?
- Where is the value of CI for teachers, administrators, students?
- What is the risk for the administration?
- Where will the groups meet?

Our initial CI was supported because the administrator at the time actively sought innovative solutions to educational problems. The second set of groups was approved by the next administration because the first group had been successful. None of the three administrators sought a formal report, but they were aware of each inquiry's progress through informal conversations with the inquirers.

CI meets the expectations of various oversight bodies for professional development—state, regional, or local—that emphasize high performance. Teacher development through CI can be linked directly to new skills that are directed toward increasing student scores on standardized examinations, but the link does not promise specific competency-based outcomes. CI's strength is that it is contextually and temporally adaptable. There has never been a union issue associated with our CI groups.

As the initiator, my responsibility involves laying the inquiry groundwork, including organizing the groups and providing for a supportive context. But there is no reason why others could not assist with issues such as the number of teachers in each group, the number of groups, possible questions, possible meeting times and places, duration of study, or record-keeping of group progress. Some of our group members have come to assume that I will continue to perform certain functions. My experience is that the more direction I assume during early stages of the process, the more difficult it is to extricate myself from being looked upon as the "owner" of CI.

Collaborative Inquiry as an Institutional Learning System

When implemented as a process of professional development in a setting such as a school, CI is an intervention into a social system and culture. In effect, we are striving to create a liberating structure (Fisher and Torbert, 1995), or container, within which learning can take place. Because of the relatively small size of our school and the porous boundaries of CI (Bray, 1995), CI becomes a learning system within the school.

Participation and Membership. I believe an open invitation and voluntary association are necessary for authentic participation. At the beginning of each inquiry year I invite all of our school's teachers to join in collaborative inquiry. Participation is voluntary. When our groups form, each member commits to be in her or his group for an academic year.

What motivates our teachers to become collaborative inquirers? Some teachers are inquisitive about new processes and want to try a new approach. They are intrigued by CI and want to "try it out." Others mention personal commitment to the initiator, reporting that they joined the inquiry because of their high regard for my leadership abilities. Often our inquirers state they are willing to try anything different from the standard approach of expert-directed workshops. Finally, teachers are motivated by previous CI experience. With few exceptions, those who have been in a collaborative inquiry group want to experience the process again.

Although potential attendance issues exist, our groups have never experienced problems. We enjoy virtually 100 percent attendance at all meetings for all inquiry groups. This high level of attendance is in part the result of negotiated school release time either in full- or half-day blocks. However, the attendance record also reflects commitment by each group member to the other inquirers, as well as the effectiveness of this learning strategy in serving participants' needs. The compelling nature of the group's inquiry question is critical as the "glue" binding the group together.

Although attrition or addition of members has not been an issue, there is one notable exception. On their own, two groups' members dissolved their groups to reform one new group, which ultimately changed the structure of the middle school. Although participants deemed their inquiry successful, some remaining members of the original two groups, not in the middle school, were unfortunately left to fend for themselves. Though both they and I tried to form a new group, they accomplished little because of the timing of their being "marooned."

Inquiry Questions. Believing that there are both good and inadequate inquiry questions, I advocate a few minimal criteria. First, a good question should be of keen interest to the inquirers. Second, inquirers must be able to take action related to their question to learn their way out of contextual dilemmas. Third, a good question is one for which the answer is not already known. Finally, if groups are asked to produce validated results for outside authorities, a good question will still meet the first three criteria. Administrators may need to "buy into" the teachers' question, but they should neither dictate the question nor control the inquiry's organic process.

One of our groups had no burning inquiry question. These teachers wanted to investigate the CI process itself. They met, determined their needs, found a question to which they could all relate, and proceeded to experience a productive and rewarding CI. The process itself was revelatory.

My experience is that question evolution is a marker of group learning. As the inquiry proceeds the group alters its question based on learning gleaned from its actions. New actions partially answer and further refine the question. Being aware that the question is likely to evolve helps groups mark their growing insights.

Action, Reflection, and Validity. In working with an inquiry group during my initial experience, I emphasized the CI criteria that make it different from other in-service models. I also encouraged the group to review our process at the end of each inquiry session. I continue to follow this process. Although each inquiry is different, *examining the inquiry itself is essential*. We ask ourselves questions similar to these: How is it working? How effective are our devil's advocates? Is everyone included? Is consensus overt and clear?

Each group varies in the rhythm of actions and reflective discussions. Although some actions appear obvious at the outset, lines of demarcation between reflection and action often blur. Our experiences sometimes lead us to ask ourselves, Was that action? Or was that reflection? For example, our first inquiry group's initial action was to find out what we knew about ourselves vis-à-vis our question, *How can we improve our practice as teachers?* Each teacher carefully noted teaching practices between meetings. These actions produced the grist for group reflection, which helped us delineate whether we thought our current practices were useful, ineffective, or of uncertain value. Based on our reflective insights, we tried out new practices on which we reflected while acting. This process helped us understand the difference between action and reflection and at the same time how the distinction can blur.

The amount and depth of the critical reflection generated by CI in teachers' inquiry groups is surprising. Our inquirers have grown more comfortable with questioning assumptions and integrating critical reflection into their professional lives. For example, the inquirers just described came to realize that they had never looked for the assumptions and presuppositions that guide their practice. In one round of reflection, they discovered the value they all placed on humor in their classrooms. Analyzing why humor seemed important, they led themselves toward hunches about the importance of seeming human and vulnerable to students. These developing hunches were tested with new actions in their classrooms.

For us, validity and evaluation concerns address the question, *Who needs to know what and what will they accept as proof?* Some knowledge produced by a group is solely for its own consumption; inquirers' growing depth of understanding is in itself validating. For the members themselves, changes in their professional lives provide a powerful indicator of inquiry validity. This form of validity is based largely on whether or not actions work. Other groups may have to prepare reports of validated findings.

In our small community, discussions about CI often occur outside of the reflection sessions. Our groups become organic units—learning communities. Chance meetings at school, grocery stores, and community events or planned get-togethers at coffee shops prior to formal inquiry sessions provide opportunities to enhance the sense of community among members. This sense of community assists with allaying distress during meetings and also fosters professional interaction outside the CI structure. For example, two members met to integrate history and science activities for middle school students. Their action facilitated further group growth.

Facilitation of Multiple Groups

Our multiple-groups design raises numerous issues. Since I cannot be in every group, I choose a group with an inquiry question of interest to me, just as any other member would. As project initiator, I am also concerned about assisting other groups with the inquiry process. Throughout my experiences as both a member and initiator, I have avoided becoming overseer of the process. I am in frequent informal contact with all of the groups but exert no authority over them.

My efforts are supported by a cadre of teachers who participated in our first CI group. When our new inquiry groups reassembled at the beginning of the new school year, mixes of experienced inquirers and those yet to be in a CI group occurred. The members with previous experience faced the same difficulties that I confront as the initiator. The task of assuring new inquirers that they can and should be on equal footing with more experienced colleagues involves clearly indicating how the inquiry process works and emphasizing that everyone has the same information vis-à-vis the inquiry question. After a few meetings, former inquirers are able to assure the newer members that they no longer possess any knowledge about CI that the newer members do not know.

In most school settings, if CI is used for teacher development, multiple groups will be necessary. Multiple groups raise the issue of how communication among groups or group members will be accomplished. Although we have no formal structure for exchanging information, each group is very interested in the progress of other groups. Participants often ask members of other groups about processes and progress. For us, a formal system for exchanging information that required additional meetings would be perceived as too time consuming and therefore problematic. If we did not enjoy the active informal exchange of information we might pursue another course of action to ensure information exchange.

From Initiator to Inquirer

Being "just one of the inquirers" has been more difficult than I imagined at the outset. As a full participant I find it difficult to move from initiator to equal colleague and contributor because my colleagues often defer to me. I find that the sooner and more completely I can become a full and equal participant the better. My approach to leadership is to try to model being a solid group member. I believe that if I were to withdraw from voicing opinions in hopes of obliging the group to accept responsibility for the process, I would be abdicating my leadership responsibility.

From time to time our inquirers look to me, as the initiator of these groups, to resolve issues. When faced with questions outside of the group, I consistently bring them back to the group for discussion. For our teachers, becoming a team member involves as much or even more learning about effective group participation as it does about the inquiry topic itself.

One concern that I'm thankful remains in the rear of my mind is whether the need for distress facilitation exceeds any group's ability to allay that distress. Our groups' work with diverse issues about which members may have firmly held views creates distress in some inquirers. To date, we have not exceeded any group's ability to alleviate or set aside distress, but the potential for trauma remains.

Among distress-producing issues are reaching consensus, authentic versus marginal participation, frustration with the pace of the inquiry, side groups, perceived unevenness of the "playing field," lack of clarity in action, tacit approval followed by second thoughts, and personality clashes. Issues that frequently become stumbling blocks are a teacher's status as a veteran or beginner, or a teacher's curriculum assignment to core subject or elective. The veteran teachers or core teachers need not have expressed a higher opinion of themselves to create perceived inequities. My experience is that newer teachers and noncore teachers fear that a perception of inequality exists in others' minds. Fortunately, collaborative inquiry equalizes the inquirers as the process proceeds. For example, a physical education teacher thought his contributions might be received as less worthwhile because he did not teach a core subject. As the inquiry proceeded he came to see that he functioned as an equal member in relation to the inquiry question about how teachers could improve their practice.

Effect on the Teachers

Our teachers consider CI their opportunity to be self-determining professionals. By design, CI integrates teacher action with reflection. It allows us to choose among issues of greatest concern and provides mechanisms to guide our active pursuit of answers. Repeatedly teachers state that CI is the best development opportunity to which they have ever been exposed. Teachers look forward to their CI meetings as an opportunity to find solutions and to be reinvigorated. One inquirer joked that CI is better than drugs.

Preeminent measures of our successes with CI are the refinement of actions, learning, and changes in our professional lives. Every group modifies its inquiry question as it progresses toward solutions to workplace challenges, thus integrating new learning into question refinement. Successes of the first group led to the success of a subsequent inquiry cycle with multiple groups and multiple questions.

We find that teachers in learning groups need to understand the nature of the adventure upon which they are embarking. It is an inviting path, an evolving journey of creating an organic entity—the learning community. As collaborative inquirers, our teachers eagerly enter unfamiliar territory and experiment. As they practice their profession in relative isolation, working in collaborative inquiry groups provides a unique experience. During discussions, they often state that they have previously not known what other teachers think. Despite years of "working together" they have never really worked together. One participant put it this way: "I've worked in this school for twenty years. Until CI, no colleague has ever seen my teaching or helped me think about what I am doing." Because CI has provided a first genuine experience of working together, many of our teachers now have improved working relationships with their colleagues.

Our learning has not been confined to our professional lives; it permeates the whole of each educator. Inquirers find CI to be both invigorating and messy: invigorating because inquirers find energy when they thought they had none; messy because it is not formulaic—the way has to be found. There are many forks in the path, but only one choice at each fork can be pursued.

Frustration levels sometimes run high. One inquirer reported that she found the sessions very distressing and often cried after meetings. "It's a good thing," she said, "that the meetings are so valuable. Getting through each meeting takes immense commitment."

Coherent group action is necessary to achieve systemic change. Our educators need to interact to learn their way out of the contextual and temporal problems of our workplace. Hence our teachers learn to function in a consensually directed group, research collaboratively, and make progress in resolving their inquiry questions.

Perceptions about the pace of the inquiry vary. Teachers who believe they are benefiting greatly from CI perceive the pace of investigation as rapid. Others, who perceive the process as slow, are troubled by the intrusion of ancillary issues. I have come to believe that teachers' perceptions about the pace of the inquiry have more to do with their learning styles than progress with their question. For me, involvement in a CI group is the optimum way to gain knowledge about pace and the need for careful consideration of choices affecting inquiry pace.

In forming inquiry groups, our teachers create organic units in which each member becomes an integral part. For us, the development of group learning is necessary for effective professional development and systemic change. Each solution introduces several new considerations that are subsequently met by CI. Getting started is probably the most difficult task.

Concluding Remarks

Our school culture evolved through the use of the CI process, but there are four specific areas left for us to examine. First, we are interested in the possibility that the CI model might be altered to fit heterogeneous groups. Groups with a cross-section of administrators, board of education members, teachers, aides, and students might congregate to address a question of common interest. Actions taken by different constituencies would necessarily be different and diverse yet would still be aimed at a common resolution to a group-related problem. Second, we need further investigation of federated models for multigroup investigations, that is, where a member of each inquiry group is also in a central group to facilitate communicating among the groups for everyone's benefit. Third, we need greater understanding of virtual inquiry communities and how they might be similar to, as well as different from, face-to-face inquiries. Isolated practitioners with like interests in distant school settings could find CI a reinvigorating opportunity. For a rural school, such as ours, this may prove to be a benefit. Finally, distress facilitation needs to be examined further. What should groups and individual inquirers do when distress becomes more than anyone in the group can allay?

The presence of collaborative inquiry in our school has changed the school culture and climate. Now enjoying more action-reflection and contextually sensitive learning, our teachers uniformly agree that CI is an extremely worthwhile staff development venture. They have learned to question practices and assumptions in ways they had not done before. They function together in ways not before experienced. Potential initiators stand on the verge of creating an organic enterprise, one of group learning among professional educators. The benefits greatly outweigh the costs.

References

Bray, J. "The Noetic Experience of Learning in Collaborative Inquiry Groups—From Descriptive, Hermeneutic, and Eidetic Perspectives." *Dissertation Abstracts International, 56* (7), 2524. University Microfilms No. AAC95–39779, 1995.

Fisher, D., and Torbert, W. R. *Personal and Organizational Transformations: The True Challenge of Quality Improvement.* London: McGraw-Hill, 1995.

Glenn Commission. *Before It's Too Late: A Report to the Nation from the National Commission on Mathematics and Science Teaching for the 21st Century,* 2000, [http://www.ed.gov/americacounts/glenn/report.doc].

JOHN N. BRAY is a staff development specialist and secondary school teacher in upstate New York who has established several collaborative inquiry groups with teachers for the purpose of improving their practice and workplace environment.

10

Discerning insights from the cases, the editors comment on presentational knowing's pivotal role in learning from experience, the reciprocity between personal development and social action, and structural issues to consider when facilitating CI.

Learning from the Inquiries: Lessons for Using Collaborative Inquiry as an Adult Learning Strategy

Lyle Yorks, Elizabeth Kasl

As the preceding chapters attest, collaborative inquiry is a powerful method for facilitating adult learning. This is not surprising, given that CI principles embody adult education principles. CI is democratic, honors multiple ways of knowing, meets conditions widely held to be necessary for free and open discourse, links learning to lived experience, values action, and is often emancipatory in its intent. Derived from an epistemology of research, CI's explicit attention to validity procedures supports critical subjectivity as learners make meaning from their experience. Finally, many adult learners are intrinsically attracted to working collaboratively as a balance to the isolation and fragmentation experienced in other areas of their lives.

The eight case chapters describe myriad facets of CI that adult educators should consider when initiating and facilitating this process. Among the many issues that emerged for us as we exchanged drafts with the authors and engaged in dialogue about the evolving meaning we discerned from our collective experiences, we are choosing to discuss four: (1) the pivotal role of presentational knowing, (2) relationship between personal development and action in the world, (3) relationship of the adult educator to the group and to the inquiry question, and (4) supportive structures for helping inquirers and adult educators practice the CI method skillfully.

In our discussion, we refer to the inquiries by specific names. Table 10.1 provides a ready reference to the six inquiries conducted by individual groups and the two multiple-groups projects.

NEW DIRECTIONS FOR ADULT AND CONTINUING EDUCATION, no. 94, Summer 2002 © Wiley Periodicals, Inc.

Table 10.1. Overview of Inquiry Participants and Purposes

Chapter	Initiator	Participants	Inquiry Question
2	Suzanne Van Stralen	Nursing managers	How do we communicate in order to promote a culture of mutual respect and cohesiveness among management and staff from all departments, shifts, and facilities?
3	Linda L. Smith	Community women	What are the ways we can lower the barriers to peer counseling?
4	Annette Weinberg Zelman	Intuition group	How can we promote or nurture intuition?
5	Whitney Wherrett Roberson	Midwives	From the abundance of my heart, soul, mind, and body, how can I contribute to the conception and nurture of learning communities that empower and transform?
6	Penny Rosenwasser	Jewish women	How does internalized Jewish oppression manifest in us, and what are strategies for resisting and healing from this oppression?
7	Cecilia Pritchard, Pamelaia Sanders	Women of Color scholars	What does it mean to be socially engaged, spiritually full Women of Color scholars?

Multiple Group

Chapter	Coordinator	Project Name	Project Purpose
8	Linda Sartor	White inquiry	To develop understanding about being a member of the dominant group and translate that understanding into new behavior
9	John N. Bray	Teacher development	To facilitate professional development and improve individual teacher practice

The Pivotal Role of Presentational Knowing

Our understanding of CI (Kasl and Yorks, 2002) rests on an extended epistemology conceptualized by John Heron and Peter Reason (Heron, 1992, 1996; Heron and Reason, 1997, 2001). Four complementary ways of knowing—experiential, presentational, propositional, and practical—should be in interactive balance as learners engage their whole selves in making meaning from experience. Most of this volume's chapters provide multiple illustrations of how the four ways of knowing complement one another to provide pathways into wholistic knowing.

As adult educators whose traditional academic training predisposes us toward overreliance on critical discourse and analytic forms of knowing, we have come to appreciate particularly the pivotal role played by presentational knowing. We share our insights into the many different ways that presentational modalities function.

Presentational Knowing Evokes Experience. We note several examples in which groups evoke the experience they are trying to study. For example, the intuition group in Chapter Four was not interested in analytically describing intuition, but in gaining an enhanced awareness of it and validating it as an important element in members' ways of knowing. The group used video, film, a Brahms concerto for violin, and reproductions of paintings to evoke intuition. Verbal exercises, written or spoken, designed to assess intuition struck participants as inappropriate for their needs. Similarly, the nursing managers in Chapter Two valued guided visualization as an aide for making a transition from their hectic work environment. By ritually acknowledging the need to walk away from their fast-paced, fragmented way of being, they evoked the experience they were trying to learn about—being more wholistic in the workplace. When the Women-of-Color scholars in Chapter Seven wanted to learn more about their sense of joy, suffering, and aliveness, they turned to the Black Angel cards. The cards are brightly colored pictures of Black female archetypes that evoke intuitive knowing about the self.

Presentational Knowing Is Pathway for Emotion. Experiential knowing is the seat of emotions, which affect people's ways of being in the world. Experiential knowing is not easily communicated, either to oneself or to one's fellow learners. When learners work with expressive processes, they often are made aware of feelings and emotions that they are bringing to the learning encounter. With increased awareness, learners are more able to create congruence between their affective states and their conceptual sense-making. For example, in Chapter Six, when Emily led the Jewish women in a tag, follow-the-leader game, the playful exuberance in the movement led the women quite unexpectedly to discovering their deep emotional yearnings for community and closeness, an experience many later described as the high point of their inquiry.

Presentational Knowing Clarifies and Codifies Experience. Inquirers commonly use presentational knowing to express experience from the action phase of the inquiry in order to assist with the process of sharing experience with co-inquirers. The nursing managers, as an example (Chapter Two), used clay sculpture to help them reflect on their first action—querying others in the workplace. The experience of reliving the action through expressing it as sculpture led the nurses to an insight that they should refocus their inquiry on themselves, not on those they managed.

Presentational expression also serves as an encapsulation of complex experience and ideas, as it did for Deena in the Jewish women's inquiry (Chapter Six). When the group developed its plan for acting in opposition to feelings of internalized oppression, Deena created a watercolor design that she used to encourage herself to "act in opposition" to her feelings of invisibility and not belonging. Her painting served as a kind of conduit through which she could reconnect with the group's insights (propositional knowing) about acting oppositionally as well as with her sense of emotional support from the group. Thus, the painting provided Deena with reflective insight and courage to act when she was away from the group.

Metaphor is a common form of presentational knowing that carries capacities to clarify and codify. The Midwives (Chapter Five) used birthing metaphors in numerous ways to aid members with understanding how to "midwife" transformative learning for themselves and others. The birthing metaphor helped them not only interpret current experience but also guide subsequent actions. Daniel, from the Multiple-Group Inquiry into Whiteness project (Chapter Eight), reports that two years after the inquiry ended, his day-to-day life is still guided by insights that his inquiry group encapsulated with its phrase, "good White person." CI groups commonly create labels or short phrases that, for them, refer to complex webs of propositional insights and thus function like metaphors, as for example the nurse managers' use of "popping conversations" (Chapter Two).

Story was used by all the groups, but in the groups whose members included women of color, story was experienced as a natural cultural practice. For the community women of Chapter Three, story provided a ground in which they created an empathic field that helped them bridge cultural and racial differences. Although the women had been a formally funded work group for over a year before their CI experience, members' interactions had been confined to subgroups based on race or language. For the Women-of-Color scholars (Chapter Seven), story helped members connect deeply not only with each other but also with larger communities of color. Through their stories about family, ancestors, and progeny yet to be born, the women recognized all these constituencies as intimate confederates in their quest for authenticity in a world dominated by White hegemony.

Personal Development and Action in the World

The case chapters reveal the reciprocal relationship that emerges between inquiring into questions of personal development or identity (an inner focused inquiry) and questions directed toward enhancing personal capacity for practice (an outer focused inquiry).

Inquiries that involve intense issues of personal identity invariably result in changes in how participants show up in various settings in the world. In part this is because taking action in the world is typically an element of the CI process, as for example Amy's action in the Jewish women's inquiry (Chapter Six). As part of the group's exploration of how members might contradict internalized feelings of marginalization and shame, Amy decided to wear the Jewish skullcap or yarmulke in public on the Sabbath. When she decided to continue this action as an ongoing practice, she noticed that her willingness to be "that visible" seemed to inspire other Jews.

Another aspect of the reciprocity between inner and outer worlds is learners' growing consciousness of their actions (or inactions) in various settings. For example, from participation in the Inquiry into Whiteness project (Chapter Eight), Eleanor and Gretchen developed new awareness of racially biased remarks and new capacities to reflect critically in the moment about how to respond. Daniel is guided daily by insights his group encapsulated with the phrase "good White person," which helps him monitor habits of thinking and behaving so that he can change them. From a Midwives discussion about hegemonic discourse and "marking" (Chapter Five), Deborah decided to notice her own marking behavior. To her surprise, she recognized that her job environment was incongruent with her values. She left her job to start her own business, in which she could more effectively act for transformation.

In working their inquiry about counseling in the clinics, the community women (Chapter Three) gradually discovered they could derive important knowledge from their own experience. As they moved from being received knowers to valuing their own constructions of knowledge, their self-esteem and sense of self-efficacy grew dramatically. Realizing their knowledge would also be valued by others, the community women re-created their identity by offering consulting services to agencies in the Washington, D.C. area. Their path of inquiry went from an outward focus of peer counseling to an empowering inward focus on personal capacities and back outward again to the larger community.

A similar pattern played out in other workplace inquiries. The nursing managers (Chapter Two) and some groups from the teacher development project (Chapter Nine) focused their first actions on their environments. In both cases, first actions led the inquirers to look more carefully at themselves. Based on new insights from changes in personal capacities, they then acted to change their workplaces in ways they would not have anticipated at the onset of their inquiries.

Finally, the Women-of-Color scholars (Chapter Seven) provide a special insight about reciprocity between identity and action in the world. They deepened their understanding that being themselves, fully and authentically, in environments dominated by other culturally based ways of being is a political act. Their inner and outer worlds are intertwined in cultural praxis.

Educator's Relationship to the Group and Its Question

We perceive three models for the adult educator's relationship to the CI group. First, the educator may be a full participant in the inquiry, as in the inquiries undertaken by the intuition group, Midwives, Jewish women, and Women-of-Color scholars (Chapters Four, Five, Six, and Seven, respectively). Second, the educator may be a partial participant or an external facilitator, as with the nursing managers and the community women (Chapters Two and Three). These first two models are described at length by Heron (1996, pp. 40–42, 62–72). In our last two chapters, which describe the Inquiry into Whiteness (Chapter Eight) and teacher development (Chapter Nine) projects, we have examples of a third model, multiple groups coordinated by a single educator.

Educator as Full Participant. CI rests on a principle of co-inquiry in which peers learn together in equal relationship to the inquiry question and to each other. Four of our chapters describe inquiries undertaken by educators who wanted to be fully participating inquirers.

When the initiator has more knowledge about the CI process than other group members, there is an early tension between the roles of initiator and peer inquirer. The initiator seeks to integrate him or herself into the group as a co-inquirer while providing leadership regarding process. Annette and Penny in Chapters Four and Six describe their honed consciousness regarding the balance of co-participation with providing direction. While engaging the validity procedure, examining hierarchies of influence, the Jewish women explained to Penny that her voice carried more weight than others in relation to the inquiry process, though not to its content. "The content of what everyone says is heard equally," they told her. "People concede to you around process, not content." Annette, in the study of the intuition group in Chapter Four, tended in the beginning to inhibit her participation because she feared exerting too much influence. Bill Torbert helped her re-think her perception when he admonished, "All you're modeling is powerlessness." John, who coordinated the teacher development project while participating as a full member in one group, observes in Chapter Nine the importance of modeling: "Being 'just one of the inquirers' was more difficult than I imagined. . . . My approach to leadership is to try to model being a solid group member."

Whitney's experience with the Midwives in Chapter Five illustrates the need for continuing leadership and facilitation during times of transition. Over time membership in the group changed, signaling transition in the life of the inquiry. During this transition the group was unstable in terms of attendance, and Whitney missed several meetings herself. Although members eventually resolved the resulting tension, the incident illustrates the need for regular reflection on the criteria by which a group is functioning, including the relationship of the adult educator to the group. John Bray, Joyce Lee, Linda Smith, and Lyle Yorks (2000, p. 73) use the metaphor of a constitution in reference to such criteria, since they constitute a living document that finds meaning in the interpreted experience of the group.

When two people co-initiate a group, they are wise to spend considerable up-front time forging mutual understanding. Co-initiators Cecilia and Pamelaia describe in Chapter Seven two challenges. Although they eventually discovered a natural affinity in their interests, in the beginning they thought them different—Cecilia's in social activism as a spiritual path, Pamelaia's in being an African American scholar. Most challenging was their exploration of what it means to be Women of Color. Many intimate and honest exchanges led to Pamelaia's changed perception about Cecilia, whose appearance has afforded her with white-skin privilege.

Educator as External Facilitator. Among the six chapters describing single inquiry groups, the first two are examples of inquiries in which the initiator is not a fully participating member. Sometimes a CI group invites an outsider to facilitate its work. Such is not the case in these two examples. Both initiators approached organizations, hoping to recruit groups who would engage questions that they themselves found compelling.

Suzanne Van Stralen (Chapter Two) has strong interest in the fragmentation and separation she witnesses in the many workplaces she has served as a consultant. Consequently she periodically joined the nursing managers in their reflections, evoking her own experiences. However, her intention was not to become a full member of the group and her focus was on facilitating the nurses' inquiry as an intact management team.

Linda Smith's relationship with the community women is more complex (Chapter Three). Linda's original vision was an inquiry that addressed social marginality and empowerment, and she expected to be a member of the group. Because the community women did not initially understand Linda's abstract presentation of the issue, they settled on a more concrete topic about their practice as peer counselors for breastfeeding. As she is not a mother, Linda could not participate. However, the women's marginal social status resonated with Linda from both her early experiences and her work as an adult educator in community development. As the inquiry evolved from its focus on peer counseling to personal empowerment, Linda became more of a co-inquirer.

Linda's experience raises issues that are fundamental for all adult educators with social change agendas. Finding herself in a position often experienced by participatory action researchers, Linda perceived a need that the community women did not initially recognize. Her experience illustrates a process in which the adult educator seeks to articulate an emancipatory interest while remaining open to the possibility that the group will not choose to evolve in this manner.

Both Linda and Suzanne worked actively to assist their groups with taking responsibility for their own learning. Linda describes "waiting and watching" for the opportunity to encourage the community women to ask questions. She began this inquiry with the epistemological framework of *Women's Ways of Knowing* (Belenky, Clinchy, Goldberger, and Tarule, 1986) as her guide, knowing that she wanted to lead women who were accustomed to being received knowers toward an epistemology of constructed knowing. Suzanne created an intentional strategy for developing self-direction. For example, over the course of the group's first five sessions, she systematically added new elements of responsibility, until by session seven group members were fully in charge of planning and facilitation.

Educator as Multiple-Group Coordinator. The third model is of great interest to adult educators because it provides a vision of how educators can leverage CI as a learning process for numbers of learners larger than those with whom the educator can participate directly. We explore this model as we take up the issue of providing structure for inquirers.

Creation of Supportive Structures

As both the above discussion and the preceding chapters suggest, conducting a CI group is a potentially challenging, as well as energizing, experience.

Support for the Co-inquirers. Fully exploiting the potential of CI is a challenge, in part because groups unfamiliar with the process can easily drift into some other form of activity. In Chapter One we described how two participatory principles, in combination, make CI unique as a research or learning process. Adults in this culture generally are not used to perceiving that their learning can be derived from their own experience and that they can share all decisions in planning and carrying out a learning strategy. Further, the educational establishment's tendency to privilege analytic thinking and propositional knowing leaves many adults unskilled in engaging multiple ways of knowing. Most adults also require skilled help with the distress that arises from emotional trauma connected to the topic or with interpersonal conflict.

Educator's Checklist. Because the elements that define the CI process are so countercultural, providing guidance for the methodology should be part of the adult educator's responsibility. Although CI is an adaptable structure that cannot be reduced to a list of prescribed behaviors, we recommend a kind of "checklist" to help inquirers monitor their process. We note these essential elements: (1) framing an appropriate question, (2) using the lived experience of group members as the basis for learning and meaning-making, (3) implementing cycles of action and reflection, (4) maintaining authentic peer relationships, (5) working with multiple ways of knowing, (6) providing for distress facilitation, (7) establishing recurrent examination of validity procedures, (8) agreeing on criteria that will guide the group's work.

Absorbed as a collective whole, the case descriptions in this volume offer insights into all these elements, as do the seminal reference works by Heron, Reason, and Bray with his colleagues, which are cited throughout. Space limitations prevent us from summarizing those insights here.

Multiple-Group Coordination. When the educator is not present in the inquiry group, as in the case of multiple-group coordination, we urge imaginative pursuit of supportive structures. In the Multiple-Group Inquiry into Whiteness (Chapter Eight), the structural mechanisms—such as reflection papers, on-line exchanges, and the representative planning committee—help Linda Sartor in her role of "shepherding" the groups. These mechanisms allow her to stay in touch with what is happening in the groups and provide indirect guidance on occasion. More concretely, the planning committee itself serves as a sounding board in which representatives from the various groups can surface issues and discuss them.

These same mechanisms, along with an end-of-year symposium, play a dual role. Providing a larger sense of learning community, they help leverage the learning from what is essentially a federated design.

Contrasting with the Inquiry into Whiteness, the teacher development project does not have a complex supportive infrastructure. Once the groups are organized, John joins one of them as a co-inquirer. Because of the school's small size, group members can easily make use of John's experience, although he is very reticent about providing explicit direction. Sharing among groups also occurs, facilitated by the small size of the school and local community. How such dynamics would work in a larger, more complex setting is an open question.

Bootstrapping. . . . or Not. Heron (1996, pp. 40, 62) has suggested that CI groups might "bootstrap" themselves into existence without the help of an experienced educator. He notes that although such a group fails to benefit from experienced guidance, it also is free from the hazard of remaining dependent on its initiator and thus never developing authentic peer relationships. We realize that we ourselves participated in just such a bootstrapping experience when we launched our first project in 1991, guided only by Reason's 1988 edited book. Our inclination is to recommend the merits of having experienced inquirers in the group—either as initiators-facilitators or as peers. We note that both of the multiple-groups projects benefited from having group members who had previous experience with the CI process.

Support for the Educators. Although the issue is not taken up in the chapters themselves, we believe it important to explain the structures that supported the adult educators in these projects. All of the initiators' understanding of CI is influenced in some way by the context of graduate studies. Whitney (Chapter Five), who was a seminary student, had learned about CI from Elizabeth Kasl. Although she did not study in the graduate school where Elizabeth is faculty, Whitney initiated her inquiry as an independent study project at the seminary and used Elizabeth as a sounding board and coach during its early stages. Suzanne (Chapter Two), Penny (Chapter Six), Cecilia and Pamelaia (Chapter Seven), and Linda Sartor (Chapter Eight) all took a formal course in which they practiced CI in practicum format under Elizabeth's supervision. Suzanne, Penny, and Linda later used the method for their dissertations, with ongoing consultation from Elizabeth during the inquiry process. Annette (Chapter Four), Linda Smith (Chapter Three), and John (Chapter Nine) also used CI in dissertation work. They, along with two student colleagues, met in seminar fashion for three years as they planned, conducted, and made sense of their CI experiences (thINQ, 1993; Group for Collaborative Inquiry and thINQ, 1994). The kind of support that can and should be provided in such seminars has been described by Reason and Judi Marshall (2001), who have developed deep expertise in their pioneering program at the University of Bath, where graduate student research is experience based and action oriented.

Although we do not believe it necessary that adult educators undertake CI in the context of graduate study, we do believe the supportive structures experienced by the authors of these case chapters is a necessary ingredient for successful CI. We strongly suggest that educators who develop CI practices form seminar groups and arrange for experienced coaching.

Other Important Issues

Many other important issues are suggested in the case chapters. We mention two briefly.

Influence of Gender, Education, Race, or Culture. We acknowledge that nearly all participants in the inquiries described here are women. The only men are in the multiple-groups projects, in addition to one nursing manager and one intuition group member. The only group that includes some participants without postsecondary education is the community women (Chapter Three). Five groups are predominated by White, middle-class life experience. From our perspective, the influence of gender, education, race, and cultural background on participants' experience of CI is a topic that needs to be explored. Any patterns discerned from this collection of experiences is limited but can be suggestive for future research.

Initiation of CI in Organizational Settings. We believe that CI has great potential for adult development in organizations or other institutional contexts. However, the participant autonomy required by CI raises issues that must be negotiated. First and foremost is the freedom of the inquiry group to pursue its own question within the parameters of a general purpose. Institutional stakeholders must agree that inquirers have freedom to control and evolve the inquiry. The space, time, and right to participate must be held sacred. Expectations about "deliverables," to use a term with currency in today's organizations, must be clear. As it is the experience of the participants, not external reporting, that is the purpose of the inquiry, any expectations about external documentation should be addressed prior to putting the group together. The effectiveness of an inquiry is defined by how it changes the learners, although inquiries will often result in changes being advocated and implemented in the organization, as in the case of the nursing managers' inquiry (Chapter Two) and the teacher development project (Chapter Nine).

A Theoretical Coda

This volume describes the practice of CI, providing rich illustration for adult educators who want to develop pedagogical skill with the method. We think it important to mention that this pedagogy is based on a theoretical point of view different from the one that guides most North American adult educators.

Experience has long been held to be a cornerstone of adult education practice, providing the medium through which learning occurs. Although it has been widely acknowledged that people encounter their experiences as whole persons (Dewey, 1958; Miller and Boud, 1996), the dominant view is also that these encounters only become "experience" when infused with conceptual or reflective thought (Boud, Cohen, and Walker, 1993; Mezirow, 1991). This is the basic position of pragmatism, which ends up privileging discourse and dialogue, pointing away from other forms of knowing.

In contrast, CI is based on an epistemology that is rooted more in phenomenology than pragmatism (Heron, 1992). With a focus on the lived phenomenon of experience, which is replete with feelings and tacit knowing, CI offers fresh perspective on how educators can help adults learn from their experience. We believe that this epistemology helps meld the reciprocal relationship between personal development and action in the world that is found in these cases.

Closing Note

Collaborative inquiry is a powerful strategy for facilitating communicative and personally emancipating adult learning. Application of CI can occur in a wide variety of settings. In initiating an inquiry, whether as a full participant or an initiating educator, the adult educator should approach the strategy from a position of learning. This chapter has touched on some of the challenges and issues that we have learned about from working with the authors of these inquiries. Bringing these observations into the public arena has been an important objective of our project. Our hope is that this volume stimulates further discourse among adult educators on the use of CI.

References

Belenky, M., Clinchy, B., Goldberger, N., and Tarule, J. *Women's Ways of Knowing.* New York: Basic Books, 1986.

Boud, D., Cohen, R., and Walker, D. "Introduction: Understanding Learning from Experience." In D. Boud, R. Cohen, and D. Walker (eds.), *Using Experience for Learning.* Buckingham, England: Society for Research into Higher Education and Open University Press, 1993.

Bray, J., Lee, J., Smith, L. L., and Yorks, L. *Collaborative Inquiry in Practice: Action, Reflection, and Making Meaning.* Thousand Oaks, Calif.: Sage, 2000.

Dewey, J. *Experience and Nature* (2nd ed.). New York: Dover, 1958 (originally published in 1929).

Group for Collaborative Inquiry, and thINQ. "Collaborative Inquiry for the Public Arena." In A. Brooks and K. Watkins (eds.), *The Emerging Power of Action Inquiry Technologies.* New Directions for Adult and Continuing Education, no. 63. San Francisco: Jossey-Bass, 1994.

Heron, J. *Feeling and Personhood: Psychology in Another Key.* Newbury Park, Calif.: Sage, 1992.

Heron, J. *Co-operative Inquiry: Research into the Human Condition.* Thousand Oaks, Calif.: Sage, 1996.

Heron, J., and Reason, P. "A Participatory Inquiry Paradigm." *Qualitative Inquiry,* 1997, 3 (3), 274–294.

Heron, J., and Reason, P. "The Practice of Co-operative Inquiry: Research 'with' Rather than 'on' People." In P. Reason and H. Bradbury, (eds.), *Handbook of Action Research.* Thousand Oaks, Calif.: Sage, 2001.

Kasl, E., and Yorks, L. "An Extended Epistemology for Transformative Learning Theory and Its Application Through Collaborative Inquiry." *TCRecord Online* [http://www/tcrecord.org/Content.asp?ContentID=10878], 2002.

Mezirow, J. *Transformative Dimensions of Adult Learning.* San Francisco: Jossey-Bass, 1991.

Miller, N., and Boud, D. "Animating Learning from Experience." In D. Boud and N. Miller (eds.), *Working With Experience.* London: Routledge, 1996.

Reason, P. (ed.). *Human Inquiry in Action: Developments in New Paradigm Research.* Newbury Park, Calif.: Sage, 1988.

Reason, P., and Marshall, J. "Working with Graduate Research Students." In P. Reason and H. Bradbury, (eds.), *Handbook of Action Research.* Thousand Oaks, Calif.: Sage, 2001.

thINQ. "Adult Learning Through Collaborative Inquiry." In D. Flannery (ed.), *Proceedings of the 34th Annual Adult Education Research Conference.* University Park: Penn State University, 1993.

LYLE YORKS *is associate professor of adult education at Teachers College, Columbia University, where he is director of the Adult Education Guided Intensive Study (AEGIS) doctoral program.*

ELIZABETH KASL *is professor of transformative learning at the California Institute of Integral Studies in San Francisco and a founding member of three learning collaboratives.*

INDEX

Back Issue/Subscription Order Form

Copy or detach and send to:
Jossey-Bass, A Wiley Company, 989 Market Street, San Francisco CA 94103-1741

Call or fax toll-free: Phone 888-378-2537 6AM-5PM PST; Fax 888-481-2665

Back issues: Please send me the following issues at $27 each
(Important: please include series initials and issue number, such as ACE90)

1. ACE _____

_____

_____

$ _____Total for single issues

$ _____ SHIPPING CHARGES: SURFACE

	Domestic	Canadian
First Item	$5.00	$6.50
Each Add'l Item	$3.00	$3.00

For next-day and second-day delivery rates, call the number listed above.

Subscriptions: Please ❑ start ❑ renew my subscription to *New Directions for Adult and Continuing Education* for the year 2____ at the following rate:

U.S.	❑ Individual $65	❑ Institutional $135
Canada	❑ Individual $65	❑ Institutional $175
All Others	❑ Individual $89	❑ Institutional $209

$ _____Total single issues and subscriptions (Add appropriate sales tax for your state for single issue orders. No sales tax for U.S. subscriptions. Canadian residents, add GST for subscriptions and single issues.)
Federal Tax ID 135593032   GST 89102 8052

❑ Payment enclosed (U.S. check or money order only)

❑ VISA, MC, AmEx, Discover Card # _____ Exp. date_____

Signature _____ Day phone _____

❑ Bill me (U.S. institutional orders only. Purchase order required)

Purchase order #_____

Name _____

Address _____

_____

Phone_____ E-mail _____

For more information about Jossey-Bass, visit our Web site at: www.josseybass.com

PROMOTION CODE = ND3

in self-directed learning. Exploring context-based learning, informal and incidental learning, somatic learning, and narrative learning; the authors analyze recent additions to well-established theories and discuss the potential impact of today's cutting-edge approaches.
ISBN 0-7879-5773-9

ACE88 **Strategic Use of Learning Technologies**
Elizabeth J. Burge
The contributors draw on case examples to explore the advantages and disadvantages of three existing learning technologies—print, radio, and the Internet—and examine how a large urban university has carefully combined old and new technologies to provide a range of learner services tailored to its enormous and varied student body.
ISBN 0-7879-5426-8

ACE87 **Team Teaching and Learning in Adult Education**
Mary-Jane Eisen, Elizabeth J. Tisdell
The contributors show how team teaching can increase both organizational and individual learning in settings outside of a traditional classroom, for example, a recently deregulated public utility, a national literacy organization, and community-based settings such as Chicago's south side. They discuss how team teaching can be used in colleges and universities, describing strategies for administrators and teachers who want to integrate it into their curricula and classrooms.
ISBN 0-7879-5425-X

ACE86 **Charting a Course for Continuing Professional Education: Reframing Professional Practice**
Vivian W. Mott, Barbara J. Daley
This volume offers a resource to help practitioners examine and improve professional practice, and set new directions for the field of CPE across multiple professions. The contributors provide a brief review of the development of the field of CPE, analyze significant issues and trends that are shaping and changing the field, and propose a vision of the future of CPE.
ISBN 0-7879-5424-1

ACE85 **Addressing the Spiritual Dimensions of Adult Learning: What Educators Can Do**
Leona M. English, Marie A. Gillen
The contributors discuss how mentoring, self-directed learning, and dialogue can be used to promote spiritual development, and advocate the learning covenant as a way of formalizing the sanctity of the bond between learners and educators. Drawing on examples from continuing professional education, community development, and health education, they show how a spiritual dimension has been integrated into adult education programs.
ISBN 0-7879-5364-4

ACE84 **An Update on Adult Development Theory: New Ways of Thinking About the Life Course**
M. Carolyn Clark, Rosemary J. Caffarella
This volume presents discussions of well-established theories and new perspectives on learning in adulthood. Knowles' andragogy, self-directed learning, Mezirow's perspective transformation, and several other models are

assessed for their contribution to our understanding of adult learning. In addition, recent theoretical orientations, including consciousness and learning, situated cognition, critical theory, and feminist pedagogy, are discussed in terms of how each expands the knowledge base of adult learning.
ISBN 0-7879-1171-2

ACE83 **The Welfare-to-Work Challenge for Adult Literacy Educators**
Larry G. Martin, James C. Fisher
Welfare reform and workforce development legislation has had a dramatic impact on the funding, implementation, and evaluation of adult basic education and literacy programs. This issue provides a framework for literacy practitioners to better align their field with the demands of the Work First environment and to meet the pragmatic expectations of an extended list of stakeholders.
ISBN 0-7879-1170-4

ACE82 **Providing Culturally Relevant Adult Education: A Challenge for the Twenty-First Century**
Talmadge C. Guy
This issue offers more inclusive theories that focus on how learners construct meaning in a social and cultural context. Chapters identify ways that adult educators can work more effectively with racially, ethnically, and linguistically marginalized learners, and explore how adult education can be an effective tool for empowering learners to take control of their circumstances.
ISBN 0-7879-1167-4

ACE81 **Enhancing Creativity in Adult and Continuing Education: Innovative Approaches, Methods, and Ideas**
Paul Jay Edelson, Patricia L. Malone
The authors discuss innovations in a variety of continuing education settings, including the Harvard Institute for the Management of Lifelong Education; a drug and alcohol prevention program; and a college degree program developed through the collaboration of the Bell Atlantic Corporation and a consortium of community colleges.
ISBN 0-7879-1169-0

ACE79 **The Power and Potential of Collaborative Learning Partnerships**
Iris M. Saltiel, Angela Sgroi, Ralph G. Brockett
This volume draws on examples of collaborative partnerships to explore the many ways collaboration can generate learning and knowledge. The contributors identify the factors that make for strong collaborative relationships, and they reveal how these partnerships actually help learners generate knowledge and insights well beyond what each brings to the learning situation.
ISBN 0-7879-9815-X

ACE78 **Adult Learning and the Internet**
Brad Cahoon
This volume explores the effects of the Internet on adult learning—both as that learning is facilitated through formal instruction and as it occurs spontaneously in the experiences of individuals and groups—and provides

guidance to adult and continuing educators searching for ways to use the
Internet effectively in their practice.
ISBN 0-7879-1166-6

ACE77   Using Learning to Meet the Challenges of Older Adulthood
James C. Fisher, Mary Alice Wolf
Combining theory and research in educational gerontology with the practice
of older adult learning and education, this volume explores issues related to
older adult education in academic and community settings. It is designed for
educators and others concerned with the phenomenon of aging in America
and with the continuing development of the field of educational
gerontology.
ISBN 0-7879-1164-X

ACE76   New Perspectives on Designing and Implementing Effective Workshops
Jean Anderson Fleming
Provides workshop leaders with the information necessary to hone their
skills in everything from planning and instructional design to delivery and
evaluation. Seasoned workshop veterans give practical suggestions to help
professionals navigate the challenges and exploit the potential of distance
learning; effectively use technology and the media; and negotiate power
dynamics in the intensity of the workshop atmosphere.
ISBN 0-7879-1163-1

ACE75   Assessing Adult LearnFing in Diverse Settings: Current Issues and
Approaches
Amy D. Rose, Meredyth A. Leahy
Examines assessment approaches analytically from different programmatic
levels and looks at the implications of these differing approaches. Chapters
discuss the implications of cultural differences as well as ideas about
knowledge and knowing and the implications these ideas can have for both
the participant and the program.
ISBN 0-7879-9840-0

ACE73   Creating Practical Knowledge Through Action Research: Posing Problems,
Solving Problems, and Improving Daily Practice
B. Allan Quigley, Gary W. Kuhne
Outlines the process of action research step-by-step, provide a convenient
project planner, and presents examples to show how action research yielded
improvements in six different settings, including a hospital, a university and
a literacy education program.
ISBN 0-7879-9841-9

ACE70   A Community-Based Approach to Literacy Programs: Taking Learners'
Lives into Account
Peggy A. Sissel
Encouraging a community-based approach that takes account of the reality
of learner's lives; this volume offers suggestions for incorporating knowledge
about a learner's particular context, culture, and community into adult
literacy programming.
ISBN 0-7879-9867-2

ACE69   **What Really Matters in Adult Education Program Planning: Lessons in Negotiating Power and Interests**
Ronald M. Cervero, Arthur L. Wilson
Identifies issues faced by program planners in practice settings and the actual negotiation strategies they use. Argues that planning is generally conducted within a set of personal, organizational, and social relationships among people who may have similar, different, or conflicting interests and the program planner's responsibility centers on how to negotiate these interests to construct an effective program.
ISBN 0-7879-9866-4

ACE68   **Workplace Learning**
W. Franklin Spikes
Increased technology, new management strategies, and reengineered and downsized organizations have caused workplace educators to rethink their craft and formulate answers to the new and immediate business issues faced by their organizations. This volume is designed to help readers examine current issues surrounding workplace learning programs and incorporate these ideas into their own professional practice.
ISBN 0-7879-9937-7

ACE66   **Mentoring: New Strategies and Challenges**
Michael W. Galbraith, Norman H. Cohen
Assists educators in clarifying and describing various elements of the mentoring process. Also intended to enhance the reader's understanding of the utility, practice application, and research potential of mentoring in adult and continuing education.
ISBN 0-7879-9912-1

ACE65   **Learning Environments for Women's Adult Development: Bridges Toward Changes**
Kathleen Taylor, Catherine Marienau
This volume explores theory and practice in adult development, adult learning, and feminist pedagogy for learning environments designed to meet women's needs.
ISBN 0-7879-9911-3

ACE62   **Experiential Learning: A New Approach**
Lewis Jackson, Rosemary S. Caffarella
This volume presents discussions of a comprehensive model of experiential learning for instructors of adults in formal educational programs. Chapters argue that linking the conceptual foundations of adult and experimental learning to actual instructional applications is key to effective practice.
ISBN 0-7879-9956-3

ACE59   **Applying Cognitive Learning Theory to Adult Learning**
Daniele D. Flannery
While much is written about adult learning, basic tenets of cognitive theory are often taken for granted. This volume presents an understanding of basic cognitive theory and applies it to the teaching-learning exchange.
ISBN 1-55542-716-2